EXPERIMENTS IN SURVIVAL

EXPERIMENTS

IN

compiled and edited by Edith Henrich

commentary by Leonard Kriegel

SURVIVAL

ASSOCIATION FOR THE AID OF CRIPPLED CHILDREN, New York

Contents

Introduction

The person with a physical handicap is so frequently known to the public only through sentimental autobiography, fund-raising sloganeering, and professional analysis that one tends to forget that he is no more and no less than a human being. In biographies and autobiographies, he is baked in a thick, sugary crust of tepid religiosity and crisis-laden sentimentality, the kind of thing that says, in one way or another, "God is my seeing-eye dog." For the professional fund-raiser, he is not a person but an "image," whose sole function is to inspire pity in the hearts and minds of his fellow Americans in order to open their purse strings. In books and articles written from one or another sociological, medical, or rehabilitation slant, he finds himself viewed in the abstract, again not as a human being but as a statistic, or as a case study, or perhaps even as an object lesson designed to convince the reader of the efficacy of the author's approach. In none of these is he permitted to see himself (or to be seen by others) as he really is, as a human being whose basic worth is simply the result of his own human attributes.

The aim of this book, on the other hand, is to enable the handicapped person to do just that, to reclaim his humanity by interpreting his own actions, fears, hopes, desires, dreams, disappointments, and problems, and to do so strictly in terms of whatever insight he himself possesses. The focus of this book is as much on the person as it is on the handicap: it is not intended either as a sermon or as a "definitive" approach to rehabilitation.

In these pages, thirty-three people, who have in common only the fact that they have had to learn to survive and to function with some sort of physical handicap, write about themselves. They, quite obviously, do not think of themselves as either a group or a

1

category; it is our hope that the reader will not arbitrarily lump them together in some particular classification designed solely for his own convenience. Their purpose is simple enough: to communicate with other people. When the reader has finished this book, he should find that the handicapped person is far different from the picture-postcard clichés by which he has been depicted in the past—that he is, above all, a *person*, albeit a person forced to live with a physical handicap. It may be that our writers will also communicate with other people who share their problems or who, for either professional or personal reasons, are especially interested in those problems; but this is a decidedly secondary, although desirable, result.

Although many of our contributors lead fairly successful lives, none of them was chosen on the basis of being outstanding. To have included such accounts as that of Henry Kaiser, who administers million-dollar industries from a wheelchair, or that of Mayor John Collins, who administers the government of the city of Boston from a wheelchair, would have radically changed if not altogether defeated the purpose of this book. Both these men, along with other unusually distinguished people, expressed their willingness to contribute. But it was finally decided not to include any material that focused on spectacular personal achievement; the individual who succeeds in the face of adversity not only perpetuates an unfortunate stereotype in the mind of the general reader but is also extremely depressing to the person of average capacity who is himself physically handicapped. Both the general reader and the victim of a physical handicap almost unconsciously assume that the achievement was made *because of* the handicap, though in fact it might be the result of factors too complex to trace and too difficult to explain. The fact is that, except for some possible vague symbolic value, an account of Helen Keller's or Franklin Delano Roosevelt's accomplishments offers little to an adolescent girl studying Braille or to a man trying to learn to balance himself on braces and one crutch as he swings the other crutch forward.

Since they are not outstanding in any overt way, our contributors may be considered "average" men and women. But in their

articulateness, in their general degree of insight, in their very ability to sit down and survey areas of their lives that were painful,
difficult, and the causes of lifelong adjustments, they are clearly
above average. Since we did not want a mere repetition of the conventional attitudes toward handicapped people, our contributors
were asked to tell the truth about themselves, to speak personally
and candidly about their handicaps and their experiences, without
attempting to force those experiences into the artificial mold of
what they thought others would like to hear; in short, to present
their personal attitudes toward their handicaps. This was the single
restriction placed upon them—that they tell the truth, and tell it
from their own angle of vision.

The problem of actually finding potential contributors proved
to be difficult. For leads, we had largely to rely upon various foun-
dations and institutions working with the physically handicapped.
This method accounted for some of the pieces in this book. Others
are simply the results of fortunate accidents. Some of the contributors were known to individuals who had heard about this project
from one source or another. A few were suggested by other contributors. Obviously, such methods of selection are haphazard and
arbitrary, but, given the purpose and limited scope of the project,
no other methods could have been more feasible.

In the final analysis, the success of this book depends upon the
degree of insight that the reader finds here. Some of our contributors have managed to tell their stories with unusual perception;
some have evidently confused insight with a certain Hollywood
bravado in the face of pain or difficulty; others have chosen to
present their stories merely in terms of what happened at a particular time, leaving the reader to draw any conclusions he may
wish. A number of people whose stories were solicited refused to
write for this book. A smaller number wrote their stories in terms
so general as to prove, for our purposes, virtually worthless. Some
of those who promised a manuscript were, for one reason or another, unable to deliver it. It is possible that these people were not
sufficiently articulate; it is possible that some of them might, upon
thinking about their material, have concluded that it was valueless
for others; it is even possible, although we know of no such actual

case, that this book's purpose was viewed as detrimental for people attempting to rehabilitate themselves.

Whatever the reason for their failure to contribute, these people must not be regarded as failures in any other sense. One of the inalienable rights of a democratic society remains the individual's right to privacy, and any contributor whose story is here told may be said to have voluntarily forfeited his own privacy. Such an attitude is, of course, to be highly valued; without it, this book would not have been possible. But it would be flagrantly unfair to suggest that public frankness be a standard of behavior expected of all human beings. Effective communication is difficult enough; it becomes even more difficult when it is centered in what was centrally painful and even traumatic in one's life. And every piece in this book derives from such a traumatic core.

To continue this introduction is unnecessary, since we do not wish to draw attention away from the contributions themselves. Whatever additional comment we have will be reserved for the "Postscript." This book is now a fact, and it is our hope that the reader will approach each piece that follows with care, understanding, and a desire to match his own honesty with that of the writers. For if their honesty is reciprocated by the reader, then the book's success, we feel, is assured. Their stories should offer the reader a new and different perspective on the individual with a physical handicap; it may even be that their stories will become the subject of the kind of speculation that could lead to beneficial results for other handicapped people.

One is tempted to conclude on a note of praise for those contributors whose stories follow. But such a note would be both dishonest and disloyal, since these people have written what they have written not in hopes of being praised but in hopes of being understood. So we shall conclude simply with the comment that, although all these writers tried to tell the truth, perhaps only some of them succeeded. But whatever truth lies between these covers is offered finally to the reader. Let him make of it what he will.

The distances which exist between all people and can never be completely traversed were somehow made much greater with each individual body sealed up in an iron lung and each individual spirit sealed up in pain and danger. We lived so closely together without any other bonds of intimacy, and we had no privacy from one another. Some of us did not live.

NORMA DUCHIN

CHAPTER **1**

Origins

To relive any moment that may be considered a turning point in one's life is a stringent demand to make of oneself, but to relive the fear and terror, the confusion and false hopes that are the bitter bench marks of the origins of a handicap is perhaps the most difficult single task of the honest writer.

All of our contributors take some cognizance of the origins of their handicaps. Those included in this section, however, focus to a considerable degree upon those early days when they were first confronted with their futures. Their narratives form the logical starting point for a book about handicapped people, for they tell of that most crucial of all times—the beginning. That first entry of the virus, the first break in the bone, the slow but steady loss of sight, these are the moments with which many handicapped people never come to terms. And behind each of the narratives included in this chapter lies the unmentionable *if*: *If* I had not gone to camp that summer, would I have taken sick? *If* I had not been in the Normandy invasion, what would my life be like today? *If* I had gone to see a doctor in time, would I still be able to see?

Some handicapped individuals spend a good portion of their lives dwelling upon the hypothetical *if* that might have changed the future. This is, of course, not only an impossible and thankless quest; it is also self-defeating. In the long run, the ability of any handicapped individual to face honestly the moment of change offers the key to his future adjustment. When, for instance, Norma Duchin relives her original encounter with the iron lung, she shows us the moment at which her life changed so completely as to be almost unrecognizable.

All the writers whose narratives are included in this section deal with more than the origins of their handicaps, and often with as much insight, but all of them write of what is perhaps the hardest thing for the handicapped individual to bring himself to tell—of how it was when his life changed permanently, when the world turned upside down, never to right itself completely.

Frank Gentile

Frank Gentile was born in Brooklyn on October 19, 1935. In September 1951, he contracted polio and spent the next two years at the New York State Rehabilitation Hospital and the Institute of Physical Medicine and Rehabilitation. Along with his rehabilitation training, Mr. Gentile managed to complete his high school education, and in September 1953 he entered Brooklyn College. At college he was active in student affairs and helped to support himself by making costume jewelry. Among his present interests are music, the theater, art, and literature; he also likes to write, paint, swim, and bowl. Now employed as a cost control manager, Mr. Gentile is single and lives with his family in Brooklyn.

Dark brown beams of wood meeting at the peak of the roof and a silver-white moon, framed by the attic window, were the only objects that I could see in the semidarkness of the night. Everything was silent. Sleep came to me slowly that night. I had just returned from camp, and my friend and I were spending a week on Long Island before going home. It wasn't the memories of that all-too-busy summer that were keeping me awake; it was a headache that kept pounding. My neck was stiff, and there was a sharp pain in my back. I was sick and had to go home.

I awoke with the early morning sun blinding me. My headache wasn't gone and, when I opened my eyes, pains shot through my head. I tried to turn toward the other cot and couldn't. My neck was stiff. As I rose from my cot, a stab of pain shot through the small of the back. My stomach began to rumble and a burning liquid came up to my mouth; I retched. The stench filled my nostrils. My eyes no longer saw the sun as orange; it was a pulsating red and black with taunting white spots, there one second and

7

gone the next. As I went over to where my friend slept, each step became a throbbing pain in the head, neck, and back.

"Jim, I'm going home. I'm sick as hell."

"Um? Okay. Seeyalaterintheweek."

The train that I boarded was a mail train. It traveled slow motion and stopped every ten minutes. The car rocked and lurched. My stomach lurched with it. Everything was throbbing, especially my head. Throb . . . throb . . . thump . . . thump! Finally, hours later, the train pulled into the station. As I walked along the platform, blurs of faces, legs, and coats moved past me. I walked slowly, very slowly.

There was a long line of people waiting at the bus stop. I stood and waited with them. Buses beeped, cars honked, trains squeaked, and a loudspeaker from the record shop behind me blared forth a jazzy tune. The bleached blonde in front of me didn't see my legs shaking, nor did she see me sit down on my baggage, exhausted. The *Wall Street Journal* man standing next to me in the packed bus didn't see the cold sweat break out over my whole body—until I started to fall.

"Are you all right?"

"I'm okay."

"Here, let me help you."

"Thanks," I replied weakly.

Then came the long three-block walk to the house. As I shuffled down the street I glanced at the surrounding houses. They began to revolve, slowly at first and then faster and faster. My head spun as I tumbled backward. The cement was damp against my back, and the sky was a dark blue. A false sense of peace came over me as I lay prone on the ground. I could not understand what was the matter with me, and no answer would come. I was too tired to panic. Eventually, I picked my weary body up and went down the block to my house.

The bed in the corner of my room looked soft and inviting. It was the only object my eyes were able to focus on. All else was a blur. I pulled my clothes off and threw them in a heap on the floor. With a full bladder I entered the bathroom. I stood before the bowl for a long time, trying to urinate, straining and running the water. Nothing happened. My hands began to tremble and I could feel the aching throb in my head become more intense. I still didn't know what was the matter. I left the bathroom with the full bladder and went to bed.

The night was long and restless. The bed, which had looked soft, was uncomfortable. The covers were tangled and lumpy. A cold, clammy sweat covered my body, flashes of heat gnawed at my nerves, and goose pimples came and went. Horses galloped through my nightmares. Their hoofbeats were the throbbings of my headache, and the steel horseshoes dug into my back. Their muscular bodies galloped over a pitch-black plain. Orange and bright yellow lightning flashed around them and through my body. They all tumbled, uttering agonizing neighs as they writhed on the ground, steel hooves cutting the air, and then all was quiet.

In the morning I awoke feeling weak. I started to reach for the shimmering glass of water on the night table, but my arm just hung limp at my side. After sitting on the edge of my bed, I rose and started to walk toward the bathroom. My legs were unsure. The left leg crumbled beneath the weight of my body and the floor came up at me. Thump! Pinned under me was my limp arm. Footsteps ran up the stairs.

"Frank, what happened?" Dad's voice pleaded.

"I'd better call the doctor," Mom said.

The family doctor's cracked leather valise sat at the foot of the bed. His kind, middle-aged face looked down at me. Solemnly he uttered his routine questions.

"Can you lift your leg? Now your arm. Where does it hurt? When did this first start?"

Who? What? When? Where? How?

Instrument after instrument found its way out of the bag, attached to the skilled hands that were performing each particular ritual. A stethoscope was at my chest. A thermometer was in my rectum. A rubber mallet tapped my joints and reflexes.

He walked out into the hall with Mom and Dad. Quiet whispers came from their direction. I heard soft sobs. He re-entered the room and I could see that his brown eyes were glistening with compassionate tears that had not yet fallen.

"Frank, I've called an ambulance. You are going to a hospital. There they can take better care of you. You're very sick. Now don't be frightened when I tell you this—you have polio."

I lay there, immobile. My semi-nude, lean body was prone on the thin slab with my arms and legs stretched out straight. Only my head was free of the cylindrical machine that surrounded me. This pukish-green iron lung with glass portholes was my demon and yet my savior. It enclosed and separated me. It breathed for me, in . . . out . . . in . . . out.

The mirror above my head was my eyes. No, it was more than that. It was an everchanging painting through which I viewed my environment, in reverse and on a flat surface. When someone spoke to me, he didn't really speak to me. He looked at and conversed with my own unique painting. I viewed these people as faces, shoulders, and voices, nothing more. Sometimes they were just mouths and necks. The passing "parades" were blurs of white smocks, masks, and caps.

Around my strange painting were beds, other respirators, white-uniformed nurses and doctors, rusty brown walls, and white bedding. White, green, brown, and more white. The only variation of this pattern could be seen through the windows. That consisted of brick-red buildings half hidden by green trees and foliage and a long, thin patch of blue sky.

To my right was the empty bed, with clean white sheets and an undented white pillow, that I had occupied before the doctor had said, "Frank, your breathing is very weak. The respirator will breathe for you until you can do it on your own."

And on the left was blonde Connie, a girl of ten who also occupied a respirator. She constantly ground her teeth.

There was the perpetual humming of motors, loud then soft, whoosh . . . whoosh; teeth grinding, crunch . . . crunch; feet moving through the corridors and from cubicle to cubicle, squish . . . squish; the whispering of voices mouthing incomprehensible sounds beneath the infrequent shouts and cries of the patients, "Nurse! Nurse!"; the stretchers and wheelchairs, squeak . . . squeak; the clatter of bedpans and urinals at all hours; and the tinkle of the dishes and silverware at meals. All these sounds made up the hospital symphony.

The loudest of these sounds were my thoughts. There was a kind of progress in them as in a musical theme. They occupied me throughout the hours that seemed like years. In the beginning, they were terse and uncertain, full of questions. Then, slowly, a theme began to develop. It went back in time and evaluated the uselessness of my past life. The notes became more persistent and meaningful. Feelings and emotions sought and found usefulness. The life I had now and the things I would be experiencing gained in significance. My mind would have to do the things my body couldn't. It would have to be more sensitive than other minds were. Would have to be? It was already. But how could I express myself? Finally, the main theme played loud and clear—paint and write, paint and write. Write! Write!

After the contagious period, I was transferred to the New York Rehabilitation Hospital in West Haverstraw. It was there, overlooking the Hudson River, that I spent the next year and a half working diligently to rebuild the muscles in my body that had remained undamaged. Not only did my body undergo rehabilitation but my mind became more acute.

This wasn't another hospital with white walls, the smell of ether, lousy food, and a businesslike staff. Every facility was available. The food was abundant and delicious. The staff was congenial. There were activities in the evening such as games, meetings, and plays. There was a Patients' Council that coordinated these activities and represented the patients to the staff.

As president of this council I had the opportunity to talk with doctors and patients. The council gave me the opportunity to see at first hand the functioning of a hospital and strengthened my notion that procedures were made for a purpose. I also talked frequently with a physical therapist on topics ranging from physiology to politics. His talks with me opened new doors through which my mind found many new paths.

After a stimulating discussion I would head straight for the library, get a book on the subject, read all or part of it, and discuss it with him the following week. Thoreau, Hemingway, and others became my close companions. I lived on a ward where there were fifty men of all ages coming from many places. This was where I gathered and stored many experiences. Some men had traveled all over the world; others had never before left their farms. There were those who had known only their immediate families, and others who had known and met famous people. I met lawyers, ditchdiggers, executives, and window washers. We complained, laughed, discussed, argued, and sometimes said nothing. It was at this time, too, that I became acquainted with classical music. There were two fellows who had records playing constantly. It wasn't long before I knew who Beethoven and Stravinsky were. Of course, there was the daily routine where I relearned how to eat, dress, and perform other activities of daily living, sometimes with the sweat pouring from me.

Just before my discharge I made up my mind to go to college. I knew this was the only way to satisfy the great curiosity that had been aroused in me about the world, past and present. It was then, too, that I became fairly certain that my self-realization would come through working with and helping others, probably the handicapped.

I arrived home in March 1953, and began to apply to local colleges for admission. Since my father was an auto mechanic and my mother a secretary, they could not afford to pay my tuition away from home. I chose Brooklyn College because I could manage the physical environment independently and live at home. I utilized my artistic ability by creating and selling costume jewelry for extra money while attending college.

Brooklyn College was another enriching experience in my life. If I had the choice of reliving my most pleasant memories, I would choose these four years. Here I enjoyed all my courses with the exception of trigonometry and Spanish. I couldn't take enough psychology, sociology, English, speech, and art. Broad horizons were opened to me which I never realized existed—Freud, White, Schopenhauer, Kandinsky, social stratification, pragmatism, abstract expressionism. I can recall working for months until all hours of the night on a paper concerning attitudes toward social class. However, it was not all work and no play: I was a member of

Alpha Phi Delta, Psychology Club, Inter-Fraternity Council, Executive Council, and other student activities. Awards and presidencies followed me in these groups as in the past.

After graduation I applied to graduate school for an advanced degree in rehabilitation counseling. I was accepted and am now attending New York University. Meanwhile I took a job as a Cost Control Clerk at Abilities, Inc. At the end of two years I was able to move up to the position of Cost Control Manager.

Norma Duchín

Norma Duchin was reared in Montclair, N.J. After graduating from high school, she studied at the Ithaca School for Dramatics and at Goucher College. She also taught tennis and then married M. G. Duchin, a lawyer who made his career in the United States Navy. While stationed in Washington in 1949, Mrs. Duchin contracted polio, which left her virtually completely disabled. She is the mother of a son and daughter.

We were living in Washington, D.C., when I contracted polio. My husband is a naval officer, and he was stationed there. I was twenty-nine years old, and we had a son and a younger daughter.

I had always enjoyed athletics so much that I had even taught tennis for a few years, and the active use of my body was so much a part of my personality and character that I was not the only one who found it hard to believe that all this active life was suddenly at an end.

I am glad that during those early, frightening weeks after polio struck I did not know that I would lose almost all my capacity for muscular movement. It had never occurred to me to worry about physical disabilities—I laughingly referred to myself at the time as a mannequin with a mind. I now recall more soberly the horde of physicians who repeatedly moved over my various parts, consulting among themselves as though I were not present. The incident I remember most vividly was provided by a young intern who explained, in my presence, "This is an example of a critical polio patient with complete involvement."

During the first months in the hospital, my greatest need was a relationship with a physician who would talk *with* me and not *about* me. I think that the shock to my nervous system, as I

14

listened to the intern's thoughtless description of my condition, was as great as any physical pain caused by my disease. I longed terribly for the competent person who would turn away from my limbs and give sympathetic consideration to my feelings and my mind.

In the room I occupied in the hospital, there were usually about eight patients. We were from different kinds of family backgrounds and from different parts of the country. What we had in common at first was intense suffering and the fact that each of us was a prisoner in an iron lung. For each of us the most important thing in the world was to draw a breath.

In spite of my earlier complaint about the intern, there was no doubt in our minds that the best doctors were exerting their best efforts to help us live. But even under these conditions it was, I suppose, one of the strangest of human communities. The distances which exist between all people and can never be completely traversed were somehow made much greater with each individual body sealed up in an iron lung and each individual spirit sealed up in pain and danger. We lived so closely together without any other bonds of intimacy, and we had no privacy from one another. Some of us did not live.

Something very good gradually began to happen to us. The feeling of being forced to live together changed all of us. We all accepted our lives as they were. The feeling of wanting not to be less brave than the person in the next bed was followed by the feeling of honestly wanting to be considerate and helpful. Then, slowly and mercifully, humor and affection grew. We became friends.

One night a close friend of mine reached the point where she was considered able to "sleep out" of the iron lung for the first time. Sleeping out for the first time is a terrifying experience for a person who has not been able to be sure of breathing without an iron lung. It is always preceded by a long training period, beginning with seconds and ending with hours. But even this careful preparation is not enough to control the fear. Having made progress in learning to breathe without help is not enough to depend upon easily in surrendering the body to many hours of sleep. The young woman, who was terrified that she would need help and not have enough breath to call for it, asked me to stay beside her in my iron lung. I recall with mixed emotions lying awake beside her all night, guarding her while she slept like a healthy youngster. I remember the day I proved to myself that I was able to breathe voluntarily for two hours, but I was certain at that time that "sleeping out" would never happen to me.

Other matters concerning my condition were less clear. I did not know or care about my muscular prognosis in the early stages, but I gradually learned, quite without anyone's spoken confirmation, that it would not be my destiny to go out and do the jobs slated for the more fortunate patients in the group. When I had improved even more, I asked my doctor whether or not I would ever walk again. His reluctance to answer me candidly made it even harder for me to understand my situation.

People generally praise us for our more obvious acts of bravery, but the moments of deep suffering are overlooked. At the hospital I had a delightful friend who spent nine months there with weak-muscle polio. She was on a different floor, and her visits, as she was mobile, did much to brighten my day. When she left, walking, I observed her departure by means of a mirror. It was truly a moment of misery for me. I had lost a friend, and I knew that I would never be leaving to step into an automobile.

Nevertheless, the two years in Baltimore gave me the growing strength to settle for an acceptance of my own limitations. Day by day, watching some victims progress beyond the point I could hope to reach and watching others not make the grade at all—this gave me perspective into my own situation. I learned to rejoice in minor advances, which in my case were in the respiratory area, and to learn, with lessening panic, that I could not move my arms or legs or spine—ever again.

To find yourself among strangers who have not shared your experiences is a wretched trial for the paralyzed person who, at first in normal society, is isolated and lonely. My hospital friends and I took care of this situation for each other. It is unlikely that any of us in Baltimore would have met or been attracted to each other on the basis of our ages or personal interests. However, learning literally to live with a group of persons who must fight the same grim and overwhelming battle was a wonderful lesson in humanity, a beginning of love. There are six surviving members of the group with whom I lived in Baltimore during those two fateful years when none of us could breathe outside an iron lung. It has proven quite impossible to forget each other. We keep regularly in touch by means of a round-robin letter. I, as the oldest, am the "big sister" of the group. We are vastly dissimilar, but we shared a memorable and solemn experience.

In a way, many things in the world might be different if people were forced to learn how much they need each other and if each of us, beset by daily woes, would come to realize how important he is to the man next door. I wonder if people all over the world will have to buckle under a common catastrophe before they learn that living together is possible—and even good.

In those days, the National Foundation for Infantile Paralysis did such an extraordinary job of helping the polio patient and his family in every conceivable way that I think the awareness of this also helped to draw us together. The government gave no funds to this organization; the people of the country gave it all. Help did not stop with hospitalization and medical and nursing care and expensive equipment. Members of the Foundation went to remote parts of the country to help individual members of the family of the patient and, when the patient was released, always followed his progress with care and whatever other kind of help was needed. I'm not sure that every foundation for disability spends its funds equally well, but this is the way we polio patients felt when we were the recipients of the benefits.

I still use the iron lung at night. I am used to it now, and I know that it is completely trustworthy equipment. The only potential danger is the possibility that electricity will fail, and so it is always important that I have on hand the necessary supply of batteries in good working order. During the day I use what is called a "rocking bed." It is not as confining as the iron lung, but it does help to relieve the strain of breathing and it gives me a real period of rest.

There is a new invention in which I am putting a lot of hope; it is an electric arm sling with a lever manipulated by the chin. The Kessler Institute, in Newark, now has orders for eight of these. If I could find a way to use one or both of my arms, it would add greatly to my independence.

I receive many suggestions from people—all kinds of ideas about how I should spend my time. The disabled always have "helpers." A while ago a *very* well-intentioned welfare worker admired my glassed-in porch and at the same instant decided that I should become a bird-watcher.

"But birds sort of bore me," I told her. "I have much more of a mind for my family and friends. I'm just not on very good terms with birds. They can come and go as they please as far as I'm concerned."

My visitor had so many reasons for my changing my views on this that I was fairly exhausted when she left. I told my mother about it, and she really put an end to the matter. "Now look here, Norma," she said in her mother-voice, "we have put up with an awful lot from you since this polio routine began. You begin talking to *birds*, and I'm finished!"

This incident reminds me of similar ones back in the hospital. Some other person wishing to do good decided to teach everyone Spanish. I did not *want* to learn Spanish, but I decided that a little of it wouldn't hurt me, and I would try to cooperate. But there was a farmer from Kansas who was simply damned if *he* would learn a word of it. He had a private revolution in his iron lung every time the Spanish teacher appeared, and it does my character no good to imagine the words he probably said to himself in order to jam the sound of the Spanish lessons. Besides, there were mechanical difficulties; when an instructor says, "Repeat after me," you can oblige much more easily if the breath you're using happens to be your own.

Then there was the doctor from Europe who was with us for a while. He decided that iron lungs were a kind of pampering which retarded the growth of the necessary strength to breathe. During his time at the hospital we lay in terror every night, afraid he would come in and cut off the electricity. However, there was always someone right on his heels to see that no harm was done.

But now, far away from the hospital experience, I can evaluate what I have learned. For it was not only suffering: it was also learning through suffering. I know that my awareness of people has deepened and increased, that those who are close to me can count on me to turn all my mind and heart and attention to their problems. I could not have learned *that* dashing all over a tennis court.

Dean Williamson

Dean Williamson was born in Montana in 1926. At seventeen, he married his high school sweetheart and enlisted as a cadet in the Army Air Forces. After his discharge at the end of World War II, he worked at a variety of jobs. At twenty-nine, he contracted polio, which left him severely handicapped. Upon completion of his rehabilitation, he moved to Missoula, Mont. with his wife and three children. They now live with his parents while Mr. Williamson attends Montana State University as a full-time student majoring in Education. He is also designing a special "wheelchair house."

It was Wednesday, September 7, 1955, and the weather was gray and rainy. We hoped that it would clear soon and we'd have a bit more of Indian summer before the winter snows began.

It would be our fifth winter at Blossburg, a tiny railroad settlement a few miles west of Helena, Montana. Blossburg was the telegraph station where the Northern Pacific Railway crossed the Continental Divide. I worked the night shift, or "third trick," as a telegrapher.

I lived with my family in a small house provided by the railroad. The winters could often be severe; snow closed the auto road for days at a time, and the temperature was once $-57°$ F. But we lived there out of choice. We had most of the modern conveniences and life was far more peaceful and pleasant in the mountains than in the hustle of the cities. Each change of the season brought new life and color to the forests—there were hunting and hiking and fishing, more than a man was able to enjoy.

My wife, Bette, was just home, recovering nicely from recent surgery. Kathy and Mike were happy to be back in the little one-room schoolhouse where the agent's wife taught as many grades as there were children. Benjy, only one year old, was with his grandmother in Missoula, a hundred miles west. Friday afternoon we'd go to Missoula, Bette would have her final postoperative exam, and we'd bring Benjy home.

I had taken a part-time job at the lime kilns down the mountain. This extra money we were saving for a vacation trip to New York City and West Point, where my youngest brother would be graduating from the Military Academy the coming June. We spent the winter evenings planning the trip—it would be a time to remember.

Thursday morning at work I answered a call on the wire. When I had finished, I had trouble reading the message I had just copied. I couldn't make my eyes focus on the print. Probably I was just tired. This was my last shift until Saturday midnight, and there would be only a few hours of work at the kilns today and tomorrow. I'd get plenty of rest.

The agent came on duty at eight A.M. and I went home. After eating breakfast and helping Bette get the children off to school, I left for the short day's work at the lime kilns. During the day, a terrific headache developed but disappeared shortly afterward when I took some aspirin. Late that afternoon, after I had finished work and the kids had arrived home, we drove the twenty-five miles to Helena, where we had dinner and went to a show. There wouldn't be much more opportunity for such things with winter coming.

I felt well and strong and happy when we went to bed that Thursday evening. Early Friday morning I was awakened by severe pains in my lower back. I lay awake until time to get the children off to school. When they had gone, I told Bette I thought we should drive in to see the doctor.

An examination failed to show anything amiss. It could be that a slight cold had settled in the back muscles, or perhaps I had strained them. The doctor taped me and gave me some pills to alleviate the pains. We drove home. The pain was nearly gone now, and when school was out, we left for Missoula. Driving seemed to soothe the sore muscles.

That same Friday evening the pains began to return. We called the family doctor. Again examination turned up nothing. The doctor gave medication for the pain and asked that I come in to the hospital in the morning for a thorough check.

Morning arrived, Saturday, September 10. My right leg seemed to be "asleep," but I could walk by locking my knee with each step. We drove to the hospital, and I limped into the admittance office. Those were the last steps I took.

Because examination and X rays showed nothing, the doctors decided to do a spinal tap. It was early afternoon now, and I had to have help in getting from the bed to the stretcher. Afterward they wheeled me to another room, to remain in isolation until they knew what it was. The pain was gone; only a numbness in my back and legs remained. I fell asleep.

Late that evening a doctor appeared. Now I'd get the answers to some questions. "Well, Doctor, what have you found?"

He was hesitant. "Well, ah—er, you have an infection in the spine."

"Infection, huh? That covers a lot of ground." What the hell! Then suddenly I knew. "You mean polio, don't you, Doctor?"

He hesitated again for a moment, then said, "Yes—yes, that's what I mean."

There it was. I had always thought I would be scared if suddenly confronted with something like this, but I wasn't. Perhaps I was already so ill that I didn't fully comprehend. Anyway, it didn't seem to matter very much.

I remained in isolation, and the time passed rather swiftly. I seemed so very tired and slept a lot. I grew steadily weaker as the infection spread. Then early one morning the crisis passed and my temperature came down to very nearly normal. I was not aware, until they wheeled it past my door, that an iron lung had been waiting just outside for several days. When my temperature had fallen to normal and remained there for a few days, I was moved to another room and visitors were allowed.

It was clear now that I would be in the hospital for some time. Paralysis was total from the waist down. My left arm and my neck muscles were very weak. Vital capacity (the measure of breath one's lungs can inhale) was very low, which meant that the chest muscles were also affected. Both bowels and bladder were functioning improperly. There was one other very curious aspect. I knew my legs were there, but I could not feel heat or cold or pain. The loss of sensation was complete from the waist down—I could not even tell what position my legs were in.

Problems began to pile up. I had asked Bette to inform the chief dispatcher and my boss at the lime plant that I was in the hospital. I didn't have to worry about my railroad job—I could have sick leave as long as it was needed. Money? The tremendous bills would take all our savings and more. Insurance did not cover "dread diseases." Sick benefits from the railroad would not last long. Where would the money come from to keep my family and pay bills? Now that I was not working, the house we lived in would have to be given over to the man who replaced me. How could my family find a place to live with no money? Could we move before snow closed the road? And where to? What if my legs didn't recover? Could I ever work again? How could I explain to the children that Daddy might never walk again? They were so young, Kathy not yet nine and Mike only seven last July. Would we ever get out into the woods again to watch the squirrels and the deer and other animals, or the trout jumping in the quiet pools? Who'd pull the sled back up the hill after a long, swift slide? Who'd trudge halfway up the slope looking for the mitten lost on the way down? And, finally, there was the question that is never answered —Why? Why did it happen to us, to me?

The problems began to work out. The local chapter of the National Foundation for Infantile Paralysis, the "March of Dimes," took over. They paid doctor and hospital bills, laboratory fees, and for drugs and physical therapy. When I was able to use it, they bought my wheelchair and, later on, braces and crutches. It took many, many dimes, and I am grateful for every one of them.

There were other things to be paid for—special nurses, small personal items, etc. Our savings lasted long enough for this and to support the family until Bette got a job. Mom and Dad insisted that Bette and the children move in with them. They had a comfortable home with spare bedrooms in the basement, and Mom wanted her grandchildren where she could look after them while Bette was working. So our personal belongings and household goods were moved—not far ahead of the snow.

The children adjusted quickly to the new situation. They liked living at Granny's house in the city. They liked their new school, too, where there were more children in one class than there had been in the whole school at Blossburg. I suspect that the sudden extra attention they received pleased them, too; as Kathy put it, "Daddy's famous now 'cause he's in the hospital with polio."

When the newness wore off, they began to wish there were hills to sled on, and they missed their old playmates and the trains going by every day. They understood that I might never walk again, and, for them, that was that. They had no pity, and for this I am glad. They were sorry, of course, and they were forever asking, "Daddy, when are you coming home?" They came to visit often, and, as one holiday followed another, the walls of my room blossomed forth with jack-o'-lanterns and witches on brooms, then turkeys and pilgrims, and then Santas and reindeer and Christmas trees.

I gained strength very slowly. Just eating a meal was a problem; it took weeks of practice before I could feed myself without spilling. Each meal was an ordeal; my gown would become soaked with perspiration, and many meals were left unfinished for lack of strength to lift the fork. Therapy was beginning to show its benefits, though, for my neck and arm began to improve. As yet there was no indication of improvement elsewhere.

Thanksgiving was coming, and a day or two before the holiday my doctor said I could go home for a little while if I felt strong enough. Did I! Everyone was delighted at my news. The day was a wonderful one. Just to be home again for a few hours was like a shot in the arm, but by evening I was very tired and was glad to be going back to the hospital. I had not realized how little stamina I had.

When Christmas came, I went home again. This time I was allowed to stay overnight. It was a time of much happiness, spent with all those dear to me. I rested well throughout the night, and the next morning was like Christmas anywhere—shouts of glee as presents were opened and wrappings and ribbons everywhere. After turkey and trimmings, we all gathered around the telephone, and before long our youngest brother called from West Point. It was really Christmas!

Continued therapy was showing results. My neck and arm were much stronger, and breathing was easier, but there was still no sign from the lower body. Spring came, and as the weather grew warmer, I began going home occasionally on weekends and, by summer, every weekend. Nearly a year had passed. September arrived and with it a new problem. I was stronger now and needed more intensive therapy. I would soon be strong enough to start using braces. The Foundation would send me to a rehabilitation center if I wanted to go. The place chosen was the Institute of Physical Medicine and Rehabilitation, a part of the famous Bellevue-New York University Medical Center in New York City.

I wanted to go. It would mean a chance to do in months what it might otherwise take years to do. The problem was the traveling. I could feed and dress myself and manage the wheelchair; I could get from bed to wheelchair and back to bed, and, with help, I could get into and out of a car. But that was all. Could my family manage without me? How long would I be away? Well, my family had proved that they could manage pretty well, and what matter how long I would be away if I could gain strength and health?

Arrangements were made with Northwest Orient Airlines for traveling and with IPMR to receive me. When the time came, my father and brother carried me aboard the plane. Bette would go with me to New York and then return. I was still worried. How would we manage when it came time to change planes at Minneapolis?

When we finally touched down, two hefty airline representatives were waiting to carry me down the ramp to my wheelchair, already unloaded and waiting. They wheeled me through the concourse, where the terminal manager met us and told us that our connecting flight had been delayed two hours. He pointed out the various facilities of the terminal and promised to see that we were put aboard.

So there had been nothing to worry about here, but how about New York? We would be two hours late, maybe more. It would be past three A.M. New York time when we arrived. Would some-one meet us, or would we have to find our own way in the biggest city in the world at three in the morning?

It was cold and windy, and drops of rain spattered now and then as we taxied up to the apron at Idlewild. The rest of the passengers had gone when two men in uniforms stepped through the door. "You Mr. Williamson?"

We had made it. Before long we arrived at the Medical Center and were led to a desk where the night nurse sat. The long trip was over.

The nurse led us down a long hall to a room with four beds. She turned on a small light. The room was a nightmare of wheel-chairs and braces and crutches. Bette put the things I would need in a locker next to the bed and then left with the nurse, who said she could return after nine A.M. I undressed, hung my clothes on my wheelchair, and got into bed.

I awakened to the sounds of breakfast being served. The room did not seem so bad in the daylight, and I began to get acquainted with my roommates. A group of doctors, nurses, and therapists made morning rounds. The doctor in charge introduced himself and the others and welcomed me. Some of them would return later, and they continued on their rounds. Shortly my roommates began departing for their various exercises and classes.

Soon one of the doctors returned. He would be my doctor from now on—that is, as long as I was satisfied. He explained how the Institute worked, what they would try to do for me, and answered my questions as best he could. I had a feeling that this wasn't such a bad place at all.

Bette remained for five days, meeting with various doctors and counselors. A program was set up for me, and I adjusted to the new routine. There were exercises and classes of many kinds: with weights, on mats, active therapy for muscle re-education, occupa-tional therapy, and counseling and testing for vocational training.

There was entertainment in the evenings and on weekends. Movies were shown two or three times during the week and there was always television. Many show people came in the evenings and staged impromptu performances. There were tickets, often free, to the current Broadway shows, ball games and other sports events, and tours of New York City and nearby areas.

My brother, now stationed near Washington, D.C., and my cousins in Connecticut visited often and I was allowed to leave the Institute on weekends. I especially enjoyed the weekend my brother took me to West Point, where I probably saw more than most civilians who visit there. On Thanksgiving Day I was a guest at my cousin's home in Connecticut. My brother and I also spent Christmas there and then drove to Boston and up the coast of Maine, returning to Connecticut for New Year's Day. I was becoming a person again.

I was ready for braces. I had heard of many disabled persons' aversion to braces, and although I was determined not to be repelled, I shuddered with pure, cold hatred and revulsion when the brace maker laid them on me to check for fit. It lasted a moment, then was gone.

Then another problem developed that was not solved so easily. I am six feet tall, and it seems reasonable that it should be only six feet to the ground. But the first time I stood in braces it was sixty feet! After a while I got used to propelling myself along through the parallel bars, but then came the day to start with crutches. Two thin strips of wood are a far cry from steel bars anchored firmly to the floor. After long hours of patient coaxing and encouragement, I was able to manage crutches fairly well, but I could not muster the courage to try it alone. As soon as the attendant stopped holding my braces, I froze to the spot. I tried and they tried. I walked without help but could not bring myself to believe it. As long as the attendant was there I felt safe, but when he stopped, I stopped. Left standing in the middle of a large room, I shook with terror, but I could not move. After some weeks I could do quite well with assistance, but alone I was helpless. There was only one solution—I had to go home.

When it was time to go, I got into the ambulance by myself, in the front between the driver and his helper. The ambulance people helped me to board the plane. Now I was completely on my own, among strangers, for the first time in a year and a half. I would change planes in Minneapolis just as before. I had only the problem I carried with me. I was going home.

We were over Lake Michigan when one of the stewardesses came and sat in the seat beside me. We would have a half hour in Chicago. Would I like to get off? It would be no trouble to have my wheelchair unloaded, and they would help me. This was tact. She knew I would be aboard till Minneapolis, and she knew I could not get into the washroom on the plane. I thanked her and explained that my particular training and the equipment I had gave me a distinct advantage in such situations. It was good to be so independent.

When we landed, my father and brother were waiting to help me, and over at the fence stood the whole family. A short drive and we were home. We drank hot chocolate and coffee and ate cookies and donuts. Everyone talked at once till long past midnight. I was really home. Daddy was home to stay.

The business of living had to begin. I would not be able to go back to my job for a long time yet, for even though I had regained strength, I had little endurance and was forced to rest frequently. Bette had a good job, though, and there would be enough money if we managed carefully.

I had to lick my fear of falling before I could plan anything else. So in a day or two I summoned courage and put on my braces. Chairs were cleared from the living room and scatter rugs picked up. My audience was lined up waiting. The children were fascinated, and everyone cheered me on. I couldn't let them down —I had to go through with it. The first step was a miserably poor one, but I didn't fall. Another, and I was still standing. Five more brought me to the wall and to safety. I turned, leaned back, and braced my crutches to rest. Perspiration alternated with goose pimples. Now if I could just make it back to my chair. The few steps back were no credit to good crutch walking, but they got me there. Then it occurred to me: how simple it would have been

in the hospital to have had my chair brought to me! I am glad I
didn't realize this sooner, for those few steps were probably the
most important I ever took.

Four years have passed since that day in September. We do the
things most families do. We have picnics in the woods and go fishing. I need help getting up and down steps and high curbs when
I use my wheelchair, and that is about all. My health continues
to improve slowly and my endurance too. I drive Bette to work
and go on to school. I attend classes at Montana State University,
where I am just another student. I expect to return to my job with
the railroad, on a part-time basis at first, after classes are out in the
spring. I am just a common man, and I expect no more and no
less of the future than does anyone.

Has my experience done anything to change my character?
This is difficult to say. It is very hard to say honestly that this is
what I was before and this is what I am now. I think that basically
I am the same. Perhaps I have learned patience and tolerance. For
instance, it is frustrating to have things moved out of reach, but
when one realizes this is not done intentionally, it becomes a matter of no consequence. A simple "please" will restore the situation.

Children—and grown-ups, too—often stare. Once this would
have embarrassed or angered me. But I find that a few words of
explanation suffice to dispel curiosity. There are those adults whom
no amount of information will satisfy, but they are a small minority. There are other problems concerned with getting along with
people, but there is no formula for solving them save being oneself.

Many persons have said, "Oh, how brave you are to have en-
dured so much." I think bravery has little to do with it. Bravery
belongs to those who love you and must stand aside, unable to do
for you the things you must do for yourself. You endure the pain
and discomfort and mental anguish because you have to. It takes a
little love, a little work, a belief in God, and the will to be a person.

Helen Ferezis

Helen Ferezis was born in the small town of Altoona, Pa., the daughter of Greek immigrants. By the time she was sixteen, her family had moved to Baltimore and she won a Maryland beauty contest. She then went to New York to begin a career as a show girl, appearing in such hits as the *Ziegfeld Follies* and *No, No, Nanette*. Later she worked as a model, became a stylist, and eventually opened her own corsetiere shop, which she ran for twenty years. In the early 1940's she became a designer and was active in this field until her illness incapacitated her.

It was nice for many years to have people tell me that I must have found the "Fountain of Youth," for I worked eight hours a day as a designer of lingerie, was able to clean a four-room apartment, have company for dinner, make all my own clothes, and even go on the road once in a while for my firm, working around the country—California twice in one year, Florida a few months, or a Connecticut town, riding trains, planes, and buses. It meant standing on my feet for hours in department stores, taking buyers to dinner, having cocktails to entertain them, all with a fine expense account. I felt I had it made. However, my life had not always been so easy, and the travels of my younger years were of a far different sort, and with much less dignity.

Before I was nine years old, about all I remember was swimming in the ocean at Coney Island where I lived, riding carousels and racer dips, and every other conceivable ride in the greatest amusement area in the world, and I spent most of my days at the beach and my nights in Luna Park, with its millions of lights and bands playing, and darting around in the crowds. I remember climbing three flights of stairs about a dozen times a day, the last climb bringing up a bucket of coal from the cellar and swiping a few pieces from the other tenant's bin.

And then one day I heard my father dragging down his old battered round-topped trunk, with Greek writing on it, bumpity bump on each step. My mother informed me that Papa was moving out and good riddance, she said. Mother got a job as a housekeeper in a hotel next door to Luna Park, and the following year she decided to work for rich people, so we packed up and took the subway into New York, where we became a part of the household for a succession of rich families, all big names in the society columns.

When I was twelve, my mother and father got together again, and after that, with my father working as a candy maker, it was Brooklyn, living in a third-floor flat, then Philadelphia, a second-floor flat, then Baltimore, a fourth-floor flat. All I remember is climbing stairs.

When I was sweet sixteen, I won a beauty contest in Maryland, and all my prizes went to Mother's head. She dragged out her trunk again and brought me to New York on the strength of a producer's request. Almost before I knew what was happening I was taking dancing lessons, and before I turned seventeen I was jumping around in all colors of tights and feathers in a succession of Broadway musical revues. When we took these shows on the road, we covered every large city in the country. I had a long run in *No, No, Nanette*, which made popular such songs as "Tea for Two" and "I Want to Be Happy," and whenever I hear these songs played today, they really bring back wonderful memories.

When talking pictures came in, shows began to be less elaborate, and there was less big money around. We stood in front of the Palace Theatre in New York and futilely declared that talkies were "only a flash in the pan—the public will never go for canned music!" But the handwriting was already on the wall. There was no future in musical revues, and since I had almost no formal education, my face and figure were my only assets. Modeling seemed to be the only answer to how to make a living. How often I wished that I had had a normal life, with a two-parents-and-a-house-to-live-in deal. But laughter was a part of me, and I laughed it off. I became a model, opened my own shop as a corsetiere, and, after World War II, I became a designer of lingerie.

Having just hit my stride in designing, entering it far later in life than most people, I loved to see my bank teller's eyebrows go up when I brought in my check on Fridays. It was a sizable one, especially in the small Connecticut town where women were not in the upper salary brackets. The bank account was no nest egg, to be sure, but it was nice to feel that I was not overdrawn for a change.

One day, on that smooth straight bank floor, I fell—over my own feet. Someone picked me up and we laughed. The next day, I fell at the factory. I fell in my own kitchen. This was very surprising, since I had always been so sure-footed. I began to avoid cracks in the sidewalk, and when I had a high curb to step up, I held onto the lamp post. Me, with my strength, walking wobbly! Sort of on the bias. My usual comment about not having some things, like a car or furs or other luxuries, had always been that I had my health, and I had been so grateful. Now I felt that perhaps old age was creeping up; but looking ten years younger than my fifty-three, tall, blonde, still getting an occasional wolf whistle, always laughing and joking; well, I was far from an old lady. And, having no family, I had planned on a job next in Holland. I had received other foreign offers and I thought that I could now see Europe.

My unsteady walking gave me the appearance of having spent too much time in some cocktail lounge, and as I went to work at eight in the morning, no wonder people looked at me and smirked. I walked around the factory holding on to the machines for balance, and my boss and the girls thought it was because of the recent fall I had had. Then I began to notice other unaccustomed difficulties. My work consisted in cutting patterns, sewing them, and draping them on a model. My right hand was becoming all pins and needles, as though it were asleep, and soon I saw that it was beginning to affect my work. I went to one doctor after another. Perhaps they knew the signs of impending multiple sclerosis but they said nothing to me.

My boss announced, one day, that I was to be booked for six

weeks into twelve cities. I began to be terrified at the thought, as every day I walked more wobbly and my right hand was becoming weaker and weaker, making it more and more difficult to cut the heavy patterns or sew or thread the needles. As I left Idlewild for my first stop, St. Louis, no one noticed anything amiss, but I knew.

I did five weeks with no mishaps except occasional falls, ruined nylons, and scraped knees, trembly from being afraid now to cross streets as I was so slow getting across. I couldn't imagine what was happening. Maybe rheumatism or arthritis or heaven knows what. An injured nerve from one of the many falls, maybe.

As a representative of one of the largest firms in the country, I had to appear chic and smart and talk fashion, but I cared less and less what women were going to wear for the 1958 winter season, whether their figures were smooth or not. I just wanted to get home, wanted to get rid of the apartment, the job, the work. But what about money? Oh yes, money. I had not saved much, having paid my mother's expenses and then, later, the funeral costs, and also having to dress expensively for the high-toned job: hairdo's, manicures, expensive shoes. Good cosmetics come high, too. I decided that I simply couldn't afford a disease, or any kind of ailment. I was all alone in this big, wonderful world and nobody could do that to me.

I knew it wasn't mental, for I had a mind stronger than two mules. I simply couldn't walk straight. I held on to things—counters, chairs and tables, even the walls. After sitting through a movie for several hours, I could hardly get back to the hotel. It was the last week of my tour—three days in Cleveland, three more in Detroit, then home. In Cleveland, carrying the umbrella in the rain, I fell and cracked two ribs. A doctor strapped me up. I laughed about being plastered, and not from too many cocktails, either.

I managed to complete the three days in Detroit and, landing back in Connecticut about the end of November, I began to make plans to quit the job, get back to New York near my friend, my dearest friend, and cry on his shoulder. I never knew what tears were before, except for some small sadnesses that come to all normal people in daily living. I figured I would get into a hospital, get this thing cured, and then pick up where I left off.

After visiting one of the most prominent neurologists in New York and finding out that I wasn't a hospital case, and still not having a name for what ailed me, except neurasthenia, which I discovered was nerve fatigue, I got another job in New York. I couldn't think about out-of-town now. Even the thoughts of the bus ride to work frightened me. I began to take cabs and even then had to get the driver to help me and listen to his advice about what his Aunt Sarah did for her arthritis.

Six months later, I couldn't walk more than a few steps, and I did enter the hospital. For two weeks, tests, tests, and more tests. I was perfectly well otherwise, laughing, joking, and making the others laugh, too. But it was so terrifying, with thoughts of only God to help me now. He always did though, and He would now. I had that kind of faith. No more job. I knew I would have to work out a new way of life. Just how or what or where I did not know. I still have not found a way to earn a living, but somehow, with Social Security disability benefits, my club running an auction for me, Blue Cross that took care of bills, and my fingers crossed, with my guardian angel still on my shoulder, I know I'll pull through.

Beyond anything else, I have an advantage over many people, and well I know that I am more than lucky. I have a friend, a fine friend, a loyal friend. I did not build this friendship in a short time but over a period of many years, over a quarter of a century. No doubt I was a good friend, too, for to have a friend you must be one. You have to work at it, never allowing a sacrifice, great or small, to stand in the way. There are acquaintances and there are friends. To say "she is my friend" or "he is my friend" should be a testimonial of great importance. Real friends are few and far between.

So I have a friend. One friend. And that is all I need. His faith, his confidence, and my desire not to fail him will give me the courage to fight on. This valuable relationship is sheer luck, I know—or maybe it's something I really deserve. Whatever it is, I am grateful.

My small hotel room, with an open door, has meant almost as much to others around me as it has to me. It is now a place for others to drop in, to chat, to unload their burdens. They keep me from being lonely. I am grateful, however, for more than this—I also know that I am often able to be of use to them.

Both healthy minds and healthy bodies may be crippled. The fact that "normal" people can get around, can see, can hear, doesn't mean that they are seeing or hearing. They can be very blind to the things that spoil their happiness, very deaf to the pleas of others for kindness; when I think of them I do not feel any more crippled or disabled than they. Perhaps in some small way I can be the means of opening their eyes to the beauties around us: things like a warm handclasp, a voice that is anxious to cheer, a spring breeze, music to listen to, a friendly nod. These people are important to me, and I like to feel that I can help them.

Aside from my work, which I have to forego, my living pattern hasn't changed much, except that I am confined to my room, cannot get out, see a movie, go to nice restaurants, visit my friends. But any other kind of living would be difficult, as I am unable to keep house, shop, clean, cook. This is the best possible kind of living arrangement, and again I am grateful. These folks I met before I became quite so disabled now come to see me, and if I lived in an apartment away from them, I know I would miss them and be terribly lonely.

Since my hand cannot create the needlework or be of much use, and my main faculties have not yet found their place, it may be some time before I discover the real use of what I have to work with. But there must be something I can do. It is a matter of time, I know, and I try to be brave. Facing everyday problems is, in itself, bravery of a sort. Time is in its ninth month, ready for the birth of an idea.

I have just been notified by the New York Chapter of the Multiple Sclerosis Society that I am to be given a wheelchair, gratis. So you see, we are not alone, any of us. Ever. There are kind and wonderful people who donate not only time but money and mercy. My wheelchair will enable me to get up on the roof for some sunshine and fresh air, to get away once in a while from my tiny room, and I go on, knowing that God still loves me, having good friends, and with faith that a remission is a faint possibility; if not, I'll find a new career.

Ralph Anslow

Ralph Anslow was raised by foster parents on a farm in New Brunswick, Canada. In 1928, when he was nineteen, he went south to New York. After a variety of jobs, he enlisted in the U.S. Army in 1929, deciding to make the army a career. He was eventually promoted to the rank of captain. In 1943, a booby trap explosion blinded him and blew off both his arms at the elbows. Surgery eventually restored partial use of the left eye and, after extensive rehabilitation, Mr. Anslow was able to matriculate at the University of Southern California. An English major, he received his B.A. in 1955 and taught creative writing until 1959. He is now Chief of the Prosthetic and Sensory Aid Division of the Veterans Administration in Nashville, Tenn.

When the mine exploded in my hand, my life was changed. Within a few seconds I was a man without arms or vision, and more than five years of hospitalization were required before I began to try to find my own way back to life.

The loss of arms and the loss of vision are so different that I feel, in order to make myself clear to my reader, I must deal with them separately, almost as though they had happened to two different men. For example, I use my artificial arms efficiently now and am probably still acquiring ease and skill with them. But the sight which was restored by surgery for a brief time is now threatened again. Human situations as different as these, psychologically and physically and even philosophically, cannot be truthfully talked about as one experience.

The first few years after I was hit, I was like a man lost in a jungle. I stumbled around, ineffectively trying to find a way back to normal living and happiness. There were advisers, but none of them was too sure of the road to follow. Some directions I followed only to find myself back at my starting point. One trouble was that my guides, professional amputees, had much more of their arms remaining and therefore they could use a more efficient type of artificial arm. What I had to find was an amputee with stumps no better than mine who had successfully adjusted himself to living without hands.

I heard of a man who lived in Buffalo, New York, an above-elbow, bilateral arm amputee who had the reputation of being the best above-elbow prosthesis-wearer in the United States. The ward doctor at Valley Forge Army Hospital gave me a month's leave to visit this amputee at his home in Buffalo. This man turned out to be a former semi-pro baseball player who had lost his arms when he was nineteen. He taught me a great many things. First he pointed out that I was not wearing the right type of arms. Then he proceeded to demonstrate how he dressed himself, drove his car, fired his furnace, shoveled snow, ate his meals, shaved, brushed his teeth, combed his hair, handled his money, and a thousand other necessary, personal details.

He said he could do everything and that I must base my rehabilitation on the premise that I was going to become completely independent. I returned to the hospital charged with suppressed energy, but my struggle, although it now had direction, proved to be a terrible ordeal. In following my plan to become completely independent, I used my artificial arms for jobs that can be done well only with strong hands. I broke my prostheses a hundred times. What a frustration to be in a hotel room alone and have your prostheses break! What embarrassment to drop a load of heavy bundles on a sidewalk and have your neighbors pick up your purchases with pity in their eyes! Still I followed my plan of complete independence, aggressively, stubbornly, and with utter disregard for the enormous waste of energy that often left me exhausted and discouraged.

This path was proving too costly in many ways. Perhaps there was a better way. I had met many amputees, all of them different from each other; but one, a professional amputee, was the opposite of my friend in Buffalo. Although he could put on the most dexterous display of skill with his hooks and was no doubt as proficient in the use of his artificial arms as any amputee anywhere, he never criticized my crude attempts to be completely independent. Instead, he pointed out that one must not waste energy on unimportant tasks that a friend might do for one with only a few motions of the hands. He told me that he did not mind getting help with his clothes or other tasks because it saved his energy and allowed him to look fresher and tidier.

Here was the other extreme of the pendulum. I saw that each man had followed a course that suited his own personality. As a result, I modified my own use of artificial arms until I was about halfway between the policies of my two examples. I stopped doing the tasks that were too hard and impractical. I looked for short cuts and easier ways to do things. Why struggle tying shoelaces when you can use elastic laces permanently tied? Most important of all, I began to spend my energy as if it were money. At home I took all the easy ways and short cuts so I would have plenty of energy left to carry on the duties of my job for eight hours a day. There are many tasks that I do only if I have to. Most of the chores I do are those that are easy and sensible to do with hooks. My frustrations are cut down to a minimum. I am happy that I have struggled to reach this far.

I have not set the world agog with my accomplishment. I am still a double arm amputee. I cannot do everything. At most jobs I cannot compete with a person who has his hands, but I have found my place in society. I know this place well, and it fits me and my problems. In order to reach it, I had to find patterns and examples to follow. I made costly mistakes—many that might have been avoided if the right guide had come along. Above all, I have learned to get along with nonhandicapped people. They are in the majority; we are the minority. Why should we ask them to adjust to our ways?

Handicapped people are so much like children in that they want to please their nonhandicapped "superiors." Their friends will ooh! and ah! about every little effort made by the crippled person but on the other hand will not really accept the cripple as an equal human being. The nonhandicapped maintain a kind of tolerant benevolence toward us and our efforts and at the same time a kind of studied resentment, especially if they are forced to compete against us in job situations. This is why I insist that the handicapped person should be trained to adjust to the reactions of the nonhandicapped majority. Let's face it! You cannot expect a village of 500 nondisabled persons to adjust its folkways, mores, and social patterns to its half-dozen cripples.

The question arises: What is the ideal plateau of accomplishments, personal independence, happiness, mental health, job success, or monetary gain toward which the seriously handicapped person should be steered? What is the use of proving one can do a job as well as a nonhandicapped person if, in so doing, one creates a world of misery and irritation for himself, his family, and friends?

After I was hit in 1943, I was totally blind. In 1944 surgery gave me travel vision (5/200). In 1947 two operations made me totally blind again. In 1948 surgery restored a good deal of vision in my left eye (20/30-3). There had never been any hope for vision in my right eye. The improvement from this last operation held up until 1958, when the doctors discovered secondary glaucoma because of the scar tissue in my eye. Medication held this in check until September 1959. Then my tension went up and up. An operation checked this last December.

To be able to see after darkness is a new life which I can describe only as resurrection from the dead world of no light, no color, no sunshine, from a dead world punctuated by sounds as a substitute for seeing.

My tension is normal now, but the struggle never quite stops. To be sure, my job goes on. But sometimes I wonder if it is worth while to continue working under great handicaps while perhaps I could concentrate more effectively on being happy and using all my energy for the fight to hold on to the eyesight I have. I could almost surely have a better chance of keeping it longer if I were not holding down a responsible position.

I know that if there is any success in my experience, it is not that I went to college or taught creative writing or became a prosthetic specialist in the Veterans Administration. My "success" is that, having been completely blinded, I fought hard to regain my vision—and I have enough of it still to write this account of my experiences.

Moses Singleton

Moses Singleton was born blind in Jacksonville, Fla., in 1913. When he was seven years old, he went to the Florida School for the Deaf and Blind in St. Augustine. He was graduated from junior college in 1933 and from the Blackstone School of Law in Chicago in 1940. As a result of his work with the blind during the past fifteen years at the Veterans Hospital in Tuskegee, Ala., Mr. Singleton has received four citations.

I speak to the readers of this book from the easy chair in my library by means of a tape-recorder. I hold the microphone in my right hand as I talk to you, and if I do not get lost in reminiscences, I will keep track of time with my Braille watch.

I was born blind, but I had what was called "discerning vision" in my left eye. This was not enough to identify objects, but I could frequently tell that they were there. When I was about three years old I remember my mother putting her glasses on me and I was able to see something moving back and forth in front of my face. I suppose now that must have been her hand. I think my mother was disturbed for my sake about my blindness.

That year we moved to Jacksonville and then to South Carolina. Memories come back to me. I used to walk down a country road enjoying smells and sounds, and someone told me what he could see as we went along. I remember going out in the woods alone. I would yell as loud as I could, and it did me good to hear the echo come back to me. People told me about snakes, but I was not afraid of them. Once a boy came to our house in a little cart pulled by a goat. I got to ride in it down the lane that ran beside our house.

When I was four we moved back to Jacksonville. I seem to re-member very well the houses I lived in, but I do not know quite how. Usually I learn about things by putting my hands on them.

When World War I ended, there was a great deal of commo-tion and celebration. That day the streets were full of noise and excitement. When I was running back home, I ran head on into an iron post. It was a very bad lick. I have had my share of bad licks. I remember too much.

In 1920, at the age of seven, I entered the Florida School for the Deaf and Blind. There were a few hard things there, although right from the start I loved to learn. Faults of mine played into my troubles. I have always taken things too seriously, and some-times my hurt is too deep. I remember too much. I do not like to fight or argue, and I do not defend myself soon enough. I endure injustice or suffering when I am in trouble. My nature does not strike back.

The first week I was in school, I was accused of lying about something. A child went outside to spit, and he missed the ground so that it was on the step. A teacher accused me of doing this. Later on someone spit in the fountain, and when the teacher ac-cused me again, I did manage to protest that I had not done it. She said I was lying, and this hurt me so much that for days I wished I could die. I guess I was homesick, too. I couldn't go to my meals that day, and I had a hard time eating my food on the days that followed.

There was another painful time. I had been asked to join a little school gang, but when I became a member of it, I did not like some of the things they were up to, and I got out. A boy named Herbert Moore, who was stronger than I was, protected me from their retaliation, but one night when he was away, sing-ing in a choir, they got me. I was taking a bath. They got me out of the tub and forced me to sit down hard on a hot radiator. I still bear the scars from this. I remember too much.

When I went home in the summer my mother was glad to see me, and she was hurt and angry at how I had got burned. I had only six more weeks with my mother before she died. I missed my mother.

My mother had given me a little book when I was still quite small, and she had said, "This is the kind of book *you* are supposed to read." I used to "play with it" because it was my book. Now I could tell that it was a New York Point primer. I remember making out the word "apple," and then knowing that I could read it. I had learned to read Braille, New York Point, and to speak the sign language of the deaf during my first year, and I began to feel the good of this learning.

When I went back to school, I was still sad because of my mother's death. Another boy had lost his mother that summer. But I began to enjoy studying more than ever. They did not let me skip grades because I was not strong, but I learned fast. Between my second and third years at school, I had an accident which punctured my left eyeball. After that my discerning vision was gone. Yet if I had to choose between blindness and deafness, I would choose blindness. Dr. Walker, our good and wise president at the school, believed the blind and deaf should live together and learn to understand each other. It is very lonely to be cut off from words people speak and from music.

In order to earn money for some of my college expenses, I sold peanuts and, at another time, newspapers. After college, I became more active in politics and music, both interests having developed during school years. I sang in churches and on various other occasions, sometimes to audiences of over a thousand people. In 1937 I sang for thirteen weeks for a local radio station; later on I began a series of lectures for this station as a public service.

Music and lecturing came so naturally to me that I carried both these activities into my work at Tuskegee when I went there fifteen years ago. I now broadcast a program called "A Citizen Speaks," and although I enjoy the classics now much more than any other kind of music, I frequently give swing programs for the veterans at the hospital.

Music always meant a lot to me, and it still does. Now I have hundreds of albums of records to enjoy. I also have several thousand books and periodicals. I receive at least thirteen Braille magazines each month, including a weekly. I also make use of Talking Books and Talking Magazines, together with Braille books from the Library of Congress and other libraries. I am a collector: poems, magazine articles, stamps, photographs, but most of all my interests center in my hi-fi, my stereo tape recorder, and my books.

I enjoy all the blessings with which I was endowed. The sound of music is sweetest of these, but I love the fragrances of nature, especially apple blossoms, and all the many sounds of the world around me. I love the taste of good foods, of pastries and condiments, and the touch of silk and fur and satin and velvet. Yes, I know I have much to enjoy.

I don't know what sort of personality I have. I really don't take stock of it much except to make sure that whatever is wrong with it doesn't interfere with my work with the veterans. My religion is a steadfast certainty which I rely upon in my work. I believe that Faith, Hope, and Charity are absolutely necessary in work like this, not the words, but the way they work out from day to day in what we do. Rules and regulations are necessary, but they are less important than the good we can do other people out of our own natures when they are harmonious and free.

Wilmer West

Wilmer West was born in Shreveport, La., in 1915 and, except for his years in the service, resided there until his recent death from coronary occlusion. In 1935 he left high school to enlist in the army. After his discharge from the army, he worked at a number of jobs in Shreveport until he was re-inducted in 1941. Mr. West last worked as a mail clerk in a Veterans Administration hospital in Shreveport.

I was in one of the first groups of draftees to leave Shreveport, and because of my previous military training, I didn't have to go through the regular basic training that the other recruits went through. I went from various army posts to Fort Dix, New Jersey, where I was assigned to an antitank company, and, after being bounced around to about two or three more army posts, I was eventually transferred to a Florida camp for amphibious training, and then on to Camp Kilmer, again in New Jersey, from where our unit shipped out. We were in a large convoy of ships and our destination was Liverpool, England. I was on the troop ship *George Washington*, a ship captured from the Germans during the First World War.

After being at sea for a few weeks, we landed in February 1944 and I was stationed in a small town in the southern part of England until the invasion. We spent most of our time in training and participating in practice beach landings and tactics. I was assigned as a gunner in an antitank-gun squad of twelve men. Our weapon was a 57-mm. antitank gun which fired a heavy, armor-piercing shell which was supposed to be able to knock out the big German Tiger tanks. The gun was usually well dug in and protected, when possible, at road blocks, in open terrain, and along all avenues of approach of enemy armored units.

46

About three days before D-Day (June 6, 1944) our company was moved to a special area where we were confined, living in tents, and surrounded by guards and assorted people from the Intelligence units. Our money was taken from us, as well as all mail and other papers which might have been of value to the enemy; our guns were waterproofed, we were issued one carton of cigarettes apiece, and I will never forget the "jawbreaker" candy that they gave us. We finally moved out on June 4th and were taken to a boat called an LCT (Landing Craft, Tank). Our boat was British, with the name "So What the Hell" printed brazenly on its side. The craft was just large enough for our gun, the twelve-man squad, the driver, and a lieutenant.

We hit the beaches of France on the morning of June 6th in about the fifth assault wave. Bodies were stacked on the beach like cordwood, and others were floating in the water like logs. We were too scared to think of anything but survival. Aid stations were set up along the beach; many trucks were burning and there was some German artillery fire falling on us. We moved out to our rendezvous point not far from the landing area. During the firing, I ran behind a French house and found a mother dog with a litter of small puppies. (I later came back to this house to get one of the puppies which I called Frenchy, and I carried him with me everywhere I went, until I was hit.) Our company moved on, eventually to participate in the liberation of the Cherbourg Peninsula.

We went from the beach to the St. Lo area, where an infantry battalion from the Thirtieth Division had been trapped and surrounded. We were near the small French town of Martin. Our gun was placed in position at a road block to protect our troops from possible German tank attack. My squad was on duty until midnight of August 12th; I'll never forget that night as long as I live. Our bedrolls were set up near a hedgerow not too far from the gun position. At midnight my squad was relieved from guard duty and we started back to our bedrolls.

Then the German bombers came. It was shortly after midnight on August 13th, and the first wave of planes dropped flares which lit up our entire area as if it were daylight. The next wave of planes carried the bombs. I was holding Frenchy, and I had just gotten to the hedgerow and lain down when the bomb hit. All I remember was that when the bomb went off, my helmet went one way and my dog went another, and when they picked me up I was sprawled on top of my squad leader, who had been blown in two. Nine of the twelve men in my squad were killed. Frenchy was dead. I had a first aid kit in my pocket, and I took some sulfa pills and injected morphine into my arm. I don't remember feeling any pain—just numbness. I could hear voices, as if in a dream, and the voices came closer and turned into a doctor and a lieutenant. They cut off the leg of my pants and I heard the doctor say, "You're lucky, all you got was a broken leg!" (His remark turned out to be the understatement of the year.) An ambulance appeared and took us to a field hospital, and at about daylight the driver told us we could smoke. I never felt any pain at that time. At the field hospital they laid me on the ground and I asked for a drink of water. The medic went to get it, and I passed out before he returned.

When I woke up, four days later, a Red Cross lady was there and she wrote a letter to my mother for me, in which I told her that I was all right and there wasn't much wrong with me. My main trouble was with breathing, because they had a large cast on me. It was so hot that I tried to bribe someone to get me a piece of ice to put down under the cast. I was taken from there to a hospital on the beach, where I stayed in a tent on a stretcher for two days until a cargo plane came and flew us to England. There they put me in a station hospital and shaved me, and gave me some ice cream made with ice cubes from the refrigerator. I was taken to a general hospital where I stayed from August 1944 until March 1945; then I was shipped back to the States.

During that time I had a number of operations. There were five holes in my bladder that had to be fixed. They gave me a spinal anesthetic and, since then, my left leg has been paralyzed. The doctor told me that I should be out of the hospital by the first of the year, and I was already planning to join the merchant marine! I didn't really know how sick I was until a boy in the next bed from me died, and a nurse very matter-of-factly told me that I was the one who was supposed to die because I was a lot sicker than he was. There was a ceremony, and a colonel came to my bed to give me a Purple Heart Medal. He said, "It gives me *great pleasure* to present you with this Purple Heart!"

After my return to the States, I was sent to army hospitals in Alabama, Texas, Tennessee, Missouri, and from there to Walter Reed Hospital in Washington, where my right leg was amputated in 1947. I spent a total of four years and twenty days in hospitals before my discharge, during which time I had well over a hundred operations. I was a bed patient for three years before they let me get into a wheelchair. Then I received a pass to go home, and was provided with a nursing aide as an attendant. I have been a wheelchair case ever since.

My right leg has been removed at the hip joint, my left leg is partly paralyzed, my right kidney is gone, and my right arm is partly paralyzed. Yet, in spite of all this, I am just as efficient as anyone who could walk or use both hands normally. I can drive a car with special attachments, I can get in and out of the bathtub without assistance, and I can swim. And, for the first time in my life, I can dance! This may sound somewhat impossible, but when I go to parties, some of the girls will hold my hands and dance, pulling and turning my wheelchair. Frankly, I never could dance and wouldn't get on a dance floor in all the years I worked in a night club. Now, when I go to parties or dances, I no longer feel self-conscious about getting onto the dance floor. I have a compartment in the back of my wheelchair which holds ice, and I use it to cool beverages so that I don't have to go back and forth to the refreshment counter every time I want a drink.

I have made several long trips in my car and attended several national conventions of the Disabled American Veterans, and when I am asked what advice I might pass on to others confined permanently to wheelchairs, I have only one thing to say—just don't get to feeling sorry for yourselves. You've got to face it and remember that you just live from day to day. Take each day as it comes. Your disability is a part of your life so just make the best of it. I also offer this advice to patients here who have the same problems to face.

My plans for the future are to keep on in my work and live my life from day to day. Continuing to work is most important to me. Not having a job to do every day is the quickest way to start feeling sorry for myself. I've always had a wild dream of hitch-hiking to New York; I don't know why, but this idea appeals to me. I just want to get out on the highway and enjoy the experience of meeting people and seeing the sights.

At one time I was asked many questions about my disability, but I don't have much of this now, since all of my friends and fellow employees are familiar with my condition. Questions about how I lost my leg used to annoy me, so I developed a stock answer that kept these people from asking further: "I borrowed some money from a loan company and they are holding my leg for security!"

And creeping into my consciousness there came a new resolution. I swore to myself that I would get even with all the theys who had done this to me. I would work. I would discard imagination for action. I would mold the fat of my body into muscle, until my body could do whatever I ordered it to do. I would carve from the lifelessness of my legs a new will. And I would show them. Above all, I would show all the theys. The hate knotted in my stomach momentarily gave way to a dry, hard rage. I would show them. I would show them all.

Leonard Kriegel

CHAPTER 2

The Encounter

Rehabilitation begins at the moment when an individual admits to himself, either consciously or unconsciously, that he is handicapped, that life as he had known it has ended, and that he must create a new life for himself. Creating that new life entails finding new techniques for existence, new methods of movement, new powers to substitute for old, new approaches to the everyday task of earning a living. It is this aspect of the life of a handicapped individual—the actual process of rehabilitation—that we have chosen to call "The Encounter." For rehabilitation is an encounter—between the individual and his handicap, between the individual and his environment, between the individual and his self—an encounter which usually dictates whether one is merely to survive or whether one is actually to live.

The eight contributors whose narratives are included in this chapter focus largely upon that process. In some cases, they rehabilitated themselves, without professional or family help; in others, they were taught how to substitute fingertips for eyes, how to adapt a profession or job to the conditions dictated by their handicaps, how to live as full a life as possible. All of them were forced, to one degree or another, to adapt their minds and bodies to new conditions of existence. And in each case a compromise between the individual and a particular goal was made. In some cases, the goal achieved was little more than survival with a modicum of physical comfort; in others, it was the kind of functioning that we call "normal."

When the process of rehabilitation is described from the handicapped person's point of view, we are made to realize that there is no set pattern, no single formula, for successful rehabilitation. Vernal Matthew, for example, was sustained by the love of his wife and the kindness of his neighbors. Leonard Kriegel, on the other hand, points to the relationship of self-pity to rehabilitation; he shows us how self-pity can pass into hatred, hatred into the desire to "get even," the desire "to get even" into strenuous rehabilitory efforts. Doris Lorenzen tells us how she has come to an acceptance of the permanency of being bedridden. What all of them have in common, however, is that they each chose to live—rather than merely to breathe.

Leonard Kriegel

Leonard Kreigel was born in New York City in 1933 and, except for two years spent as a patient in the New York State Reconstruction Home in West Haverstraw, has lived there all his life. Mr. Kriegel received his high school education at home and then went on to Hunter College, where he received his B.A. in 1955. After earning his M.A. at Columbia University, he went on to receive his Ph.D. at New York University in 1960. He is married and is at present a Professor of English at Long Island University.

On a hot, late-July day in the summer of 1946, I returned to that same Bronx world in which I had spent eleven of the thirteen years of my life. It was, as a matter of fact, almost two years to the day that I had left. I was driven home in an ambulance, the same ambulance that had once taken me away, from the New York State Reconstruction Home in West Haverstraw. I was changed both in appearance and spirit. The appearance I can give to you with ease—distance furnishes a pliable-enough indifference to physical details. I was fat, hog-fat and baby-soft, tall for a boy just turned thirteen, five feet five inches, but almost as wide as tall. My face was oval, a pattern broken only by two heavy, drooping jowls, crowned by a thick blond pompadour, which, if I am not mistaken, was the only stylish aspect of my appearance. I do not remember what I was wearing.

What I do remember is that my father and the ambulance driver carried me out of the ambulance and stood me up on the sidewalk. My father held me up while the driver placed a crutch under each arm. I stood on the sidewalk for several seconds, the still-strange wooden sticks beneath my arms, blinkingly pausing in the mid-day sun to reacquaint myself with home. My cousin Leo walked over and stood alongside me, smiling. It was then that I knew that I was home. Leo and I had grown up together. I said goodbye to the driver and began to walk, flanked on one side by my father and on the other by my cousin, the few feet that led from the ambulance to the stone steps leading into the lobby of our apartment house. My neighbors, some of whom had devoutly prayed for my recovery for two years, huddled in smiling groups on both sides of the landing, nodding their encouragement to me and to each other. Their fear matched mine, step for step, as I approached the landing, the nine stone steps passively answering my unvoiced question. I had, of course, known the answer all the way home in the ambulance—I couldn't climb them. I stood there, staring at the steps, hating them not for having defeated me but for having done it so publicly, feeling my mother's lip-biting tension from the second-story window of our apartment, even though I couldn't see her because I was afraid to look up. It was more than the remorse caused by that first public defeat. It was the recognition of my guilt, of what I had done *to them*, to my mother and father and to all those others who had shared at least a sense of my agony if not the pain that went with it. Ashamed to look at my mother, ashamed to look at my father, ashamed even to speak, I stood there and stared down at the steps, trying to work up enough anger and hatred so that I could show my shame with tears. But the tears, like so much else that day, didn't come.

I bit into my lip, a gesture of public contrition. Finally, I looked at my father. "I can't," I said, shaking my head. "I'm sorry. But I can't."

My father nodded. "You'll walk up some other time," he said, his voice peculiarly flat. "You'll learn." Again he nodded, only this time as if to convince himself. "You'll learn," he repeated. "Won't he learn, Leo?"

My cousin was standing behind me, so I couldn't see him when he answered. "Sure," I heard him say, "sure, he'll learn."

Then my father put his right arm under my right leg, the other arm under my shoulders, and someone else, I think it was our upstairs neighbor Mr. Golden, put his left arm under my left leg, his right arm around my shoulders. They lifted me, basket style, and carried me up the stairs. Leo followed with the crutches.

It took me two or three months more to learn how to walk up those stairs. Until then, I would sit on the bottom step and boost myself up with my arms, while my brother or my mother or one of my friends held my legs high in the air. But my father was only partially correct. It was not really I who learned. It was my body. It already knew, instinctively, I suppose, that the arms could do some of the things for which legs had been made. And then it found out that even the legs could learn how ingenuity can sometimes take the place of muscle.

And that was the way it was for the next four years. My body made the moves. It adjusted. It came to know its enemies—the curbstone that was just a half inch or so too high to take on the swing-through gait, the dry leaf or piece of paper lying carelessly in the street, waiting for my crutch like a booby trap, the thin sheet of ice that wasn't visible at night unless I walked slowly, eyes searching the pavement beneath me for the secret of balance, the drops of water on a marble hallway or tile bathroom, and all the other enemies that have been with me for so long now that they are almost friends, more familiar, in fact, than any friend can be.

But the enemy I remember best, the one I still dread most, strangely enough, was the one that I shared with many other adolescents who had no idea of what it was to walk on sticks and steel. And here, I must admit, it is difficult to muster enough indifference to kill the sense of shame. What, after all, can you say about boils?

I suppose you can begin by saying that boils have a simplicity all their own. If you walk on braces and crutches, a boil is simply an additional nuisance, one which, if it erupts within the armpit or where the leather straps of a brace meet your leg, confines you to bed. And that's how this next episode began: in bed with boils. It was a month before my seventeenth birthday and this time there was a boil on each knee, both of them almost ripe but not yet ready to be lanced by our family doctor. My bed was right next to the window. It was only the middle of April, but it was warm enough so that I could keep the window open and look out on what was happening in the street below. My younger brother, Abe, and several of my friends were playing stickball. Their hawking cries floated through the window like languid balloons. It was all very familiar, almost reassuring, since by now I had assumed the role of spectator as if it were to remain permanent and unalterable. It was a comfortable role and, at that time, a necessary one. In bed, I was whatever I wanted to be, transposing the reality of any situation into the fine fabric of my imagination. The sanity of a stickball game in the street below could not really touch me so long as I lived in the Yankee Stadium of my soul.

But there were still the boils. The boils ached, pitting their own reality against that of my imagination. The boils ached, contracting with a meticulous regularity. I watched as my friend, Billy Maloney, stepped up to the manhole cover that served as home plate, dropped the pink rubber ball on the ground, and then caught hold of it with the end of the stick, driving it high and deep until it bounced against the roof of the convent at the far end of the street. The boils continued to throb. Billy trotted across home plate, and, as I watched him, I became Billy, just as I might have become any of the others, just as I frequently became whoever it was necessary for me to become. But this time there were the boils. They ached, throbbing beneath the skin, taut, expectant, waiting for the knife. I tried to ignore them, but I couldn't. It wasn't the pain; there had been far greater pain over the last six years. But that had been pain with meaning—a sharp crisis, a cold anxious moment, a sudden stab of summer lightning. And then a sigh of relief, an end to pain, the cold sweat on the forehead that signaled a new beginning. But the boils just throbbed, like a neon sign automatically flashing on and off, on and off, on and off.

And then, as unannounced as violence usually comes, the reality of my imagination dropped away, to die permanently in the sudden burst of anguish and despair that heralded my realization that I would never play ball again. The boils continued to throb, and now it was as if each contraction of pain said to me, "You are a cripple. You are a cripple. You are a cripple." It was the kind of moment that I had never before permitted to invade my consciousness, a moment of total candor. It came with all of the impact of a shock, and yet, unlike a shock, embedded itself permanently within the boundaries of my existence. I *was* a cripple. Not a ball-player, not a hero, not a lover, not even an adolescent. But a cripple. It was so simple, so brutal, that truth.

My body began to shiver in a paroxysm of self-pity. Outside, the stickball game continued. My brother stood at the manhole cover now, eyeing the pink ball that he had bounced in front of him, bringing the stick around until it met the ball and drove it past the third baseman and against the red brick wall of the apartment house after ours. For the last time, I felt the sharp sting of pleasure, just as he felt it, racing from the tips of the fingers into the shoulders. And then the tears came. At first, I wept quietly, filled with self-pity because I could never again be my brother. And then I wept harder, thinking of what *they*, of what all the *theys* in the world, had done to me. I knew that *they* had done it, the *they* of God, the *they* of my mother and father, the *they* of my brother and my friends, of all the doctors and nurses who had lied to me in the hospital, of all those people who came like mendicant saviors into my apartment to lay their sloganized attempts at comfort at my feet. I wept, and turning away from the open window, I sought solace in the warm safety of the pillow.

I don't know how long I wept—a half hour, an hour, maybe more. Time no longer mattered. Time, too, belonged to their world, the world that had turned so suddenly, so viciously, against me. All I know is that, as I lay face down in the pillow, the tears slowly stopped, the spasms of anguish grew less and less frequent, until I lay there with nothing left but exhaustion and a growing knot of hate in the pit of my stomach. And creeping into my consciousness there came a new resolution. I swore to myself that I would get even with all the *theys* who had done this to me. I would work. I would discard imagination for action. I would mold the fat of my body into muscle, until my body could do whatever I ordered it to do. I would carve from the lifelessness of my legs a new will. And I would show them. Above all, I would show all the *theys*. The hate knotted in my stomach momentarily gave way to a dry, hard rage. I would show them. I would show them all.

The next day the family doctor came and lanced the boils. It was a beginning. I knew now what I had to do, having spent the previous evening examining, not dispassionately, but with that cold clarity that is among the most valuable gifts of rage, whatever assets and liabilities I possessed. A plan of action, of self-creation almost, had taken root in my mind. But it was the body, not the mind, to which I turned. My legs were lifeless. I was still as fat as a hog. But like the stone clarity that morning-after sobriety brings to a late-night drunkard, the knowledge of my arms came to me. In the arms, I would mold fat into muscle. To the arms, my will would attach itself. The fingers in my hands I would make into toes as well as fingers, the wrists feet as well as wrists, the forearms calves and forearms, the elbows knees and elbows, the shoulders thighs and shoulders. In the arms lay my salvation.

As soon as I could get out of bed, I began to exercise. For hours at a time, I would exercise—push-ups, sit-ups, lifting weights. Today, the memory of what my body did is somewhat embarrassing. And yet, if I am to keep this memoir honest, I must also confess to a warm pride that floods my very being whenever I think back to those days. The pride is for the way in which my body, especially my arms, responded to the demands I made upon it. I suppose my behavior constituted as good an example of autism as one might wish to find. In a sense, I remained in a world of fantasy. But now the fantasy permeated my every waking moment. Now the fantasy had nothing at all to do with an imaginative second life. All that I wanted was to protect the growing self that I felt within me. I needed to be left alone, to nurture the awakening power of my body, to break through all the old possibilities my imagination had offered me into the promise of selfhood.

I allowed nothing, no one, to violate that embryo of selfhood. I remember one time, lying in a pool of sweat on the linoleum-covered floor of my bedroom, when my mother entered my room, begging me in a tearful, frightened voice to come into the kitchen for dinner. I told her to get out, with all the anger that I could muster against a threat to my new existence. And then I continued my push-ups, the ache in my shoulders growing almost as quickly as the pride in my mind, until I collapsed on the floor, gasping for breath, the salt taste of my own sweat running into my mouth. And for the first time in my life, I knew what was meant by pride in oneself.

The hate carried me. It carried me all through that year. It woke me up in the morning for an hour's exercise before breakfast. It took me through breakfast, then through the hour's home instruction that constituted my only formal schooling from the eighth grade of grammar school until my freshman year in college. It stung me into two hours of brutal physical exercise after lunch. It enabled me to go for long walks through the neighborhood on the braces and crutches. It took me home for supper. And from there it sent me to Williamsbridge Oval, a city park and playground, where I spent another two or three hours on the high bars, my arms pumping for the security my soul demanded.

The fat dropped from my body, two, three, four pounds a week, like wax dripping from a burning candle. The muscles in my arms, chest, and shoulders took on definition. The jowls disappeared. The upper part of my back grew hard and confident. My wrists and forearms thickened. And then one day, perhaps six months after the birth of desire, I stood before a mirror and looked at myself, searching my image as a connoisseur of art might search a Rembrandt portrait. And, momentarily filled with gratitude instead of hate, I began to weep. My body had forged a soul.

It is now more than ten years since that warm April day a month before my seventeenth birthday. So many things have changed. The hate has died, perhaps only because there is nothing left to feed it. I still devote fifteen or twenty minutes a day to exercise (anyone who walks on his arms learns these not-too-subtle tricks of the trade, even after the first battle has ended), but the thought of once again doing what I then did fills me with a cold sense of awe at a performance which, at this late date, seems somewhat maniacal. The self I sought so desperately is within me now, burned into the substance of my soul. I live, as most of us do, in a house of bread and dreams.

I make my living as a teacher. And despite the proper air of dispassionate professional courtesy with which I listen to the hopes, anguish, and fears of my students, I frequently find myself thinking how all of us fight our lonely wars, reaching for the enviable future we all know we deserve, afraid only of the memory because to remember is to come to terms with the dreams. The process, it seems to me, is inevitable. We are, after all, neither heroes nor cowards. Such are the limitations of our humanity.

And then I think of the many times I have been told, by doctors and social workers and other people who specialize in telling one such things, how my life is an excellent example of what the power of the will can do. My own humanity is as limited as anyone else's, and so, I sadly confess, I find such praise rather pleasing. But then, after I have regained the perspective of memory, I once again am forced to admit to myself that these people are wrong, that they simply do not know of what they speak. They speak of courage and will, but survival is never really a question of courage or will. The future is a shadow already scarred by the past. We grope along, blinkers on our minds, matching the pebbles in the country of now with the boulders in the mountain of time past. It is not a question of will or courage. We are none of us Hemingways, not even Hemingway.

Still, I survived. And I am glad that I survived. Because even if survival itself is dictated by the past, it is an accident of life and not of death. At the beginning of this memoir I wrote that existence itself remains a puzzle to me. Why I survived, I do not claim to know. But I did. All I can do is to salute my body. For it was the body that chose. And the body chose well.

Doris Lorenzen

Doris Lorenzen was born in Philadelphia in 1919. Her family soon moved to New Jersey, and it was here that she contracted polio when she was eight years old. Paralyzed almost completely, she has been forced to spend her life in bed. Miss Lorenzen is a published poet, a home service worker for the Red Cross, secretary to the local adult education program, and an active member of the Lutheran Church. She has two brothers, one sister, and seven nephews and nieces.

The induction into polio's total state began in quarantine, that ward named for the limbo in which travelers learn to forget an old world and practice some of the ways of a new one. On that frontier the people an eight-year-old knew most familiarly looked foreign in compulsory gowns and masks, and strangers loomed like albino witches with flapping sleeves and only eyes for identification. To enforce separation from all that was well known and predictable there were the insulating fever, a little pain, and a mind-emptying thirst. Now the bed was made with the child in it. Food came to the mouth in awkwardly timed swoops from another's hand. A leg was arbitrarily moved by someone else. Sounds were muffled, smells markedly different. Featureless walls, and the new custom of seeing things within the outlines of a window-frame, completed the alienation. Memory of citizenship in another realm, of brothers and sister and a desk in school, faded, disappeared.

Thus quickly the border guards took up their posts. The child asked no questions. No one volunteered an excuse for this despotism. The child knew only that nothing was as it had been. The first revelation was that nothing would ever again be as it had been, and a sophisticated story at that time about the ways of a virus could not have appealed to her imagination. Even though this was her first experience with finality, she learned the set of facts easily and never needed more formal indoctrination. Indeed, she had to be deliberately patient with persons less realistic than she.

Official quarantine ended, and her innocence was restored. But then a silent agreement as strict as quarantine went into effect. At home, in bed, sitting crookedly in the chair where she was placed, she found that all objects and experiences had first to be handled, inspected, and purified by an authority before they were transferred to her. The flower had to be de-thorned, meat cut away from the bone, the core edited out of others' adventures. This policy was meant to save the child pain and embarrassment. Instead, it made a way out of this filtered, secondhand world imperative. She began her career as an opportunist by saving a few grains of sugar to lure flies to her hand and thus to re-establish contact with the dangerous and the real.

Normally endowed people claim that they need an escape from reality; the severely handicapped person knows with passionate certainty that the wish to be a part of life is the only ambition that makes any sense. True, things weren't as they had been, but then they didn't have to be. There was a way back into living, and it became her business to find it, despite invisible barbed wire.

The first of the books she read were shoddy and silly, but the search for a script to live this odd life by led to interesting, if irrelevant, explorations. Where is my likeness, the searcher asked. It was quite probably in a book, for so many people lived there, and, in any case, there was more texture, more color, in books than the clearest window glass would admit. She was consistent enough to reject fairytales. The story-writer had to try to make a flesh-and-blood world or she would settle for her own dreams. At least those first heroes and heroines pretended to a special knowledge of life and, even though they suggested impossible philosophies, they served her purpose. She still has an envy of the nineteenth-century woman as described by the nineteenth-century man, and the saint's role and the scholar's retain the power to make her wistful. The observer would have guessed she was intent upon leaving her limited world behind; instead, she was looking for more, not less, of life.

The books and the schooling, even that kind which kept teacher and pupil in unreal, detestable exile, uncovered bits and pieces for a personal plot that she could make do for a day and a night, and then another. Imitating, exaggerating, taking in, casting out, creating her own strategy as she went along, shaping herself to helplessness and being shaped by it, she felt that events were of necessity minor, matters of implication more than fact. These were the years for greedy receiving, and she converted to some use everything that came to her.

One day her mother twisted a rubber band around pen and fingers, and fingers and pen became a single tool. Now words were not only to be taken in; they could be sent out also. The newly literate adult must feel this sense of emancipation, too, for to him also it comes quite suddenly, without the long apprenticeship of first and second grades. Reading words had helped her to create a self, but that was almost a casual method, or at least haphazard, compared with writing words, with discriminating among them, choosing this one and rejecting another according to her very own decision. A word, to her, was not merely a substitute for a deed. Usually it was the only deed that was possible.

She was graduated from high school "with" her class, but since they had never seen one another before, it was a ritual without sentiment. From now on there were no imposed assignments, only the habit of reading whatever she pleased. Occasionally she visited an orthopedic surgeon. The curved spine was forced into straightness. Spidery fingers were stretched and wrists fused, but the doctors were mostly apologetic. She had known the truth since those first September days in the isolation ward, but others needed to be convinced. Once they were, she was free to return to truly relevant concerns.

She had to stay in bed all the time now. Bed was environment and climate, the simple condition that dictated all others, and, perversely, it was where she learned that if she seized every opportunity whose existence she even suspected, and if she compromised whenever she had to, she could live well enough.

Not every expedient or compromise worked. She wrote a little, poetry mostly, and it was published in obscure magazines, but she wrote those poems out of imperfect knowledge of a world that existed only for her, and she stopped when she realized that she was compounding a fraud. She tried borrowing other people's lives and continued with that form of futility long after she had proved its hurt. Then it was revealed that, whereas borrowing divides poverty by two, sharing often doubles wealth. The stipulation was that she had to be very careful about what in her she could invite others to share.

A fat and jolly man came on another errand and was surprised that the telephone wasn't alongside the bed. The day it was moved to where she could reach it was the day the border guards were vanquished forever. For the next dozen years a family business was her chief occupation. Then she, who had been fed on the indignations of Clara Barton, Jane Addams, Lillian Wald, and other minor saints, was asked to do volunteer work for a national agency that aids servicemen and their families. Requirements were a certain measure of judgment and imagination, and constant availability. The blind Milton has described that form of service. The lovely irony was that the agency's authority plus her pen and telephone combined to bring servicemen home from some of the farthest places on earth, and she could scarcely wriggle her toes.

People came to her room. Two of them were early refugees from political tyranny, and their bookish, literal English needed softening. Her pastor introduced her to a displaced person from Hungary who knew no English at all, and she undertook to tutor him. This was dress rehearsal for the time a few years later when two young men helped their countrymen tumble down an iron statue of Stalin in a Budapest square and then slipped past very real frontier patrols to remake their lives in the United States. At the moment she is repeating the experience with an adventurer from Norway. She loves the expressions of relief, on faces blank a moment before, when a mystery has been explained, loves the sound of the new tongue saying new things with a tinge of the old, and is sure that this kind of teaching is what she would have chosen if she had had many choices.

Miracles multiply according to a geometry of their own. For several years she corrected themes for an English teacher who had been forbidden to use her own eyes. Then she was asked to work for her town's adult education program, and this, too, confirmed her belief in the basic rightness of what is called chance. Septembers and Januarys are set apart now by the frantic ringing of the telephone and stacks of mail requests for registration cards. Next semester she will also be writing the publicity releases for the courses. Occasionally there is a church project she can help with. Inevitably a chief interest is the literacy programs in Asia and Africa.

A mindless subspecies of life destroyed the citadel, but the complex remnant of life that remained insisted, just as mindlessly, that a virus cannot have it all its own way. This was how a life was remade—not according to a sensible, thought-out program, but by revelation, experiment, and discovery. She had been ridiculously naive when, at the beginning more than thirty years ago, she had expected to find a guide to do all the work for her. The truth is that she could never have accepted that degree of intercession, and luckily the adventure was reserved for her. And there is still no sense of having exhausted all the possibilities. There are more discoveries to be made than the imagination can foretell. Each day has its precious, expectant quality, is potentially a birthday.

There are two scales to adjust to in such a renovated life. First, a protecting skin that seems an integral part of other people's equipment is peeled off. There is no shielding distance between the severely handicapped person and other persons and places, no limited neighborhood of concern. When you do not know the woman who lives three houses away but have sensed kinship with a paralytic in Morocco, for instance, when you do not know exactly what the street corner two blocks away looks like but do remember a picture of Trafalgar Square, then space is a fraud and boundaries are merely contrived by myopic men.

And nothing is insignificant; no event is ignored, and "event" is a redefined word. The day unaccountably dawns, and breakfast coffee and cigarette are equally miraculous. The laggard maple tree outside the window has buds only perceptibly larger today than yesterday, but even that much change is noted. Rain never irritates but is another variety of spectacle. The dialogue between creature and creator is not drowned out in a confusion of sounds, and on some days it is quite distinct. Only the very quiet one can know it goes on at all.

Granted that it is good to tear down a slum, to brew a life-giving vaccine, to teach a mountain-mover. Still God—and how can she be tentative about God?—permits smaller dispensations that are in the merciful tradition. Perhaps all lives are the total effect of only two or three events and it is mere busyness that suggests more drama. No one speaks better of his destiny than it deserves. She does not either. However, she is convinced that those who are forbidden the blazing triumphs are nevertheless given the tiny assignments they *can* manage, and their victories are different in degree but not in kind. This belief survives even that most devastating comment: "How nice that you have these ways to pass the time!"

The discipline imposed by a physical handicap is both subtle and emphatic. Subtly it shapes an attitude about the world and our connection with it that has little in common with the world's definition, sensed in all the inaccurate things it says about us. Emphatically the discipline is different from what we expected it to be. At the same time that a handicap limits choice of action in a massive way, we learn that it has really helped to state what the choices are. We may be faced with so many that we confront anarchy.

For there is a discovery that, once made, renders all else tolerable: whatever we do is a symbol of what we would do. This is the shift of emphasis that ends the isolation. Not only can *we* do no more than to let an act substitute for a more splendid act, *but no one can do more*. This is the reconciliation.

Even so grand a physical and spiritual triumph as flinging an object at the moon is a compromise.

Camille Cayley

Camille Cayley was born and raised in Hungary, where, in addition to a medical degree, she acquired one hundred medals and thirty cups as a national athletic star. Upon emigrating to the United States, she taught pediatrics at Columbia University and at the New York University Medical School and began postgraduate work in psychiatry. In 1952, she incurred almost total paralysis as a result of an accident in her home. After extensive rehabilitation, she returned to the study of psychiatry and now has a private practice in New York. She is also on the staff of two psychiatric clinics. Dr. Cayley has a son, who was graduated recently from Yale University with a degree in engineering.

During my first three months in the hospital after the household accident that eventually confined me to the wheelchair for life, I felt as Pagliacci must have felt. While I smiled, kidded, joked, and was the life of the party in front of my innumerable visitor-friends, I really wore a mask and was mortally worried about the future. The fact that I was a physician was an emotional handicap, because I knew exactly the usual outcome of a spinal cord injury. When all the visitors had left and the nurse on tiptoes had closed the door of my room, I usually exhaustedly stopped my smile of the day and permitted myself the luxury of being sad and gloomy.

During one of these gloomy evenings, my beloved housekeeper Miss Carney, who never left my bedside, turned on television. By pure accident, the *U.S.A. Canteen* was on, with beautiful, smiling Jane Froman, who could not walk alone to the stage but was propped up on the arms of two soldiers, her living crutches. Just a few weeks before my accident I had happened to see her life story in the movie *A Song in My Heart*. I had had tears in my eyes when I saw her then, and the tears rolled out in torrents now. However, there was a great difference in why I cried then and why I cried now. Then I was sorry for her, and now I was happy because I had just found the solution for the balance of my life. This was the first time since I had become paralyzed from the neck down three months before that it had ever dawned on me that "life does not end in the wheelchair." If Jane Froman could do it, I could do it too!

The next day I wrote a letter to Dr. Howard Rusk, asking him to come to see me and tell me whether or not I could be sufficiently rehabilitated to be useful again. I did not listen to my medical friends who claimed that Dr. Rusk had no time for individuals, that he was putting all his energies into the rehabilitation movement at the local, national, and international levels. I could not believe that a medical confrère could coldly reject my plea. I was right. Within twenty-four hours, before seven o'clock in the morning, a reassuring, calm, handsome, tall, and friendly man awakened me. He was accompanied by my physiatrist, Dr. Arno David Gourewitsch. He asked Dr. Gourewitsch a few questions, examined me a bit, and then, with a reassuring smile, said: "I will be glad to have you transferred to the Institute of Physical Medicine and Rehabilitation if you are willing to promise me that you won't daydream about what additional strength will come back in your muscles, but will let us build a future on what you have now. If anything more comes back, you will consider it gravy."

I was so happy that he had come, and even happier about having been accepted at the IPMR, that I hardly heard the realistic second half of his sentence. Many months later I actually understood the full meaning of those terms and conditions, but by that time I had become accustomed to getting along without gravy.

Dr. Rusk's Institute opened a new vista for me. Even though I considered myself an up-to-date physician, I had never seen a rehabilitation center before, certainly not from the vantage point of a patient.

A strenuous five-and-a-half-month sojourn followed. All the professional staff members were most cordial and helpful, but the greatest impression was made on me not by the doctors, nurses, and the other experts but by the double amputee who kept the Institute clean, running around at good speed on his wooden legs. And Eddie, the good-humored elevator operator whose arms, legs, hands, and speech were severely affected by cerebral palsy and who still was the most efficient and cheerful elevator operator I ever met, made an indelible impression on me. The beautiful secretary of the administrator at the IPMR who rolled around graciously in her wheelchair made me hope that even though I could not be as pretty and young as she was, at least I could look as well groomed in my permanent wheelchair as she did in hers.

At the Institute two important facts became clear to me. I learned that I could not return to my former specialty, pediatrics, because the children wouldn't understand why I couldn't run after them or why the syringe would fall out of my hands. But I also discovered that medicine was still open to me. Even when I had been a pediatrician, I accumulated a good bit of psychiatric training in order to understand the child behind the running nose, and I did psychotherapy with children or their parents. It dawned on me now that with a small amount of extra effort, I could complete my psychiatric training, and that the practice of psychiatry would not require the use of my helpless arms and legs but could be managed from the wheelchair as long as my mind remained intact.

But the cost of accumulating enough control analysis seemed exorbitant to me now, when my nine months of hospital and nursing bills had made me a virtual pauper. At this point, Uncle Sam came to my rescue. I learned from the vocational counselor at the Institute about the U.S. Office of Vocational Rehabilitation, which locates and finances good rehabilitation risks. Because I had been a fighter all my life, sometimes in swimming, sometimes in tennis, sometimes for democracy and against prejudice, I felt that for once I could fight for myself, too. I considered myself a good rehabilitation risk, and so did the Office of Vocational Rehabilitation. They spent $1,700 on me, and I had to prove that the taxpayer's money was well spent. So I put all that I had into my total rehabilitation, into finishing my psychiatric training and building up a private practice in psychiatry.

By 1955 I was not worried about the future, but I was worried about a moral debt which I had. I owed a lot to the world of the handicapped because it had inspired me to an optimistic outlook on life in spite of the inconveniences and hardships of being confined to a wheelchair. I chose to pay this debt by creating Courage, N.Y., Inc., an organization "for the handicapped, by the handicapped." Our goal is to expose the poorly rehabilitated to the well rehabilitated for inspirational and motivational help that may contribute to maximum rehabilitation. We want to convey to as many as possible of the poorly rehabilitated handicapped people what I learned at the Institute of Dr. Rusk: "Life does not end in the wheelchair."

Vernal Matthew

Vernal Matthew was born in New York City in 1900 and was educated there in the public schools. At an early age he began to study music. He was married in 1920 and left Columbia University, where he had been studying, in order to give private music lessons. Mr. Matthew was also the organist for the Seventh Day Adventist Church. After losing his vision, he was forced to give up music until he learned to read it in Braille. Mr. Matthew is the father of three children.

In 1951, it was discovered that I had chronic glaucoma, which cannot be helped by surgery. The disease had progressed a long time before I realized that I had to go to a doctor and find out what was the matter. I suppose that knowing the piano so well, loving music so much, having my hands on the keyboard so large a part of every day—I delayed seeking proper professional help until very little more than light perception was left to me. And my wife has always helped me in so many ways that I was spared some of the details which might have warned another person of failing vision. In any case, there was nothing which would have stopped the process, and I was forced to hear the verdict that I would soon be completely blind.

I took this about as hard as a man can take misfortune. I could not accept it with my brain or my heart—and yet I had to. Fear and hate were hard knots in my stomach. One night I went to the incinerator and burned everything that had been part of my artistic past: music I had composed for the use of my students, sheet music I most loved, books, pictures. I had enjoyed photography as a hobby, and I threw pictures I had taken into the fire. Later I gave my camera to my son, and sold the rest of my photographic

71

equipment, as well as my grand piano, at a great financial loss. It simply felt like the end of life for me.

I had a feeling of fright when I sat down in front of the keyboard. I cannot explain the reasons for this unless, perhaps, it represented for me all I had lost and could not bear to have lost.

A few bitter months passed, and my wife and I decided to use what money we had left to enlarge and winterize our little house in the country and move there permanently in the hope of earning a living raising chickens and turkeys on the seventy-five acres. The house was a small two-story frame building with two rooms on each floor—no running water, no modern facilities except electricity. We added a kitchen and bathroom and a drilled well, and later we installed central oil heating. We were located on a hill with a magnificent view stretching from the Mohawk Valley and the hills south of it to the rolling foothills of the Adirondacks on the west and north. The sunsets were unspeakably beautiful. From our hilltop the Northern Lights could be seen in the fall and winter.

In the beginning our hopes were heightened, but our venture failed. We lost our investment and had to sell our house. We had nothing left of material value. But there had been a kind of redemption during those six years in the country. My spirit had somehow, in spite of all my losses, survived. For during that time I lost myself in service to the community along the line of music, interest in which had returned with the opportunity to do something constructive. I organized a choir in the little village church, and spearheaded its effort to purchase a suitable organ. One of the bright spots in the fund-raising effort was bringing a choral group from the choir of the church in New York City where I had been organist for sixteen years. This "chorale" not only aided substantially in a financial way but was a great inspiration to our local choir. Their visit was such an artistic success that they were invited to return on two subsequent occasions. In addition to this I had the pleasure of training two organists, one each for our little church and its neighbor some miles away.

We know now that we shall not be able to have our little house again. We dream of it and speak of it sometimes, but we are sensible people and we know that it is gone.

But before we left, two dinners were given in our honor by the people of the parishes for whom I had played the organ. At one I was presented with an illuminated picture of the Last Supper; at the other, a purse. I regard these as an expression not only of appreciation but of love.

It was chiefly my wife's influence which led me to ask for advice and help from the Lighthouse after we returned to the city. As soon as they understood my love and need for music, they began teaching me music in Braille. Of course, first they had to teach me Braille itself, the ordinary written "words." But learning Braille in music is a strange and wonderful experience which I suppose many people might find hard to imagine. A student memorizes the Braille music—Bach, Tchaikowsky, Ravel, the others I love, are in my own brain now. They are part of me. They are mine as sheet music could never have been. It took time, of course, and concentration, but it was the beginning of life again. During two years of study the Lighthouse gave me a teachers' training course which equipped me to teach music to sighted people. One of the first things I did on returning to the city was to learn to type. I now use the typewriter for my personal correspondence.

I began to get my first class together only last fall; it is still small, but it is growing. Once more life is very good and music is the soul of it. Once again I am on the way to supporting my family with the work I love to do.

I do not need much sleep. I often lie for hours at night, going over the music in my mind. Sometimes I wake up in the middle of the night and study. It is mine again and in a new way. This sense of intimacy with music is, of course, hard to explain in words. Sometimes I wonder if it resembles in any way what Beethoven may have felt about his own compositions, particularly after he was deaf.

Julius Feig

Julius Feig was born in New York City in 1922. After graduation from high school, he worked in a retail hardware store and then went into the service. A combat wound necessitated the amputation of his right arm, and Mr. Feig now wears a right upper-extremity prosthesis. He is Chief of the Prosthetic and Sensory Aids Service of the Veterans Administration. In 1955, he was chosen as Amputee of the Year. He is married and has a twelve-year-old son.

Growing up in New York City did not prepare me well for roughing it in the Army. My home life had been good, even in the frugal, hardworking depression years. I had liked school and had been a good student. I had many good friends and somehow we never got into any trouble, individually or as a group. But some of my experiences in the Army were frightening and hard to take.

I was inducted into the service in 1942 when I was twenty, and in less than two years I was in the middle of it. Although we did not know it until later, my brother and I were both wounded in action on July 6, 1944. I was wounded by shell fire at about two o'clock in the afternoon, but I had to wait until six the following evening before I got any help. The front was changing hourly at this stage of the war, and it was hard for the First Aid outfits to locate all the wounded. Due to multiple injuries suffered about the face, I had lost a lot of blood by the time I was found.

At the hospital I learned that my right arm had been amputated. My left hand was also in bad shape, and both shoulders and my right eye had been damaged. Other injuries added up to a long time on the sick list. At the recuperation center to which I was sent many weeks later I met my brother who, as I have said, was

wounded the same day as I was. He was less severely injured, however, and he was able to help me with a problem which had been
troubling me a lot: how to break the news of a major amputation
to a grieving father.

Both my arms had been in splints for many weeks, and letters
home had had to be written by others. I knew that anxiety would
be building up at home because of this, but still I was not able to
write. Now my brother wrote home for me and slowly broke the
news: "Julius will not become a butcher or a laborer." I later
found out that this much knowledge of my condition was a wel-
come relief to my family. They had feared that I might have been
blinded.

I was finally returned to the United States three months later
for more recuperation and for rehabilitation at a rehabilitation
center in Atlanta, Georgia. Part of this involved the fitting of a
right hand upper extremity prosthesis and instruction in its use.
I had constantly wondered what a prosthetic arm would look like
and whether it would be recognizable from the human hand. A
group of arm amputees was brought together to be introduced to
our new physician.

He introduced himself to the group and told of the advances in
this field. He thereupon called an orderly to summon an arm amputee patient who had been fitted with a prosthetic for demonstra-
tion. I vividly recall my heart thumping, wondering whether I'd
be able to differentiate between the prosthetic arm and the human
hand. Imagine my chagrin (and also the group's) when in walked a
patient wearing a utility arm commonly called a hook! It was later
explained that more natural terminal devices were available and
could be easily interchanged on the arm. The terminal devices are
selected based upon the occupation of the wearer. A utility hook is
usually recommended for industrial work, whereas a more natural
looking hand is usually furnished to those who are engaged in
office work.

In the weeks just before discharge from the Service, my
thoughts began to turn toward the future. What occupation
should I attempt to find? I was not able now to return to the

housewares business, and it seemed important to make the right choice so that I might become independent as soon as possible and gain satisfaction from my work to balance against some of the things I had had to do without.

I remembered how people had spoken highly of Civil Service positions during the depression, and I decided to look into this possibility. Within days after my discharge on March 3, 1945, I had taken the Civil Service Examination and passed it. I was assigned to work at the Veterans Administration in New York City. I started to work on March 19th, about two weeks after my discharge; I was awfully eager to get started. I was employed in the Finance Division, where it gave me great satisfaction to prepare for payment the necessary papers to release money to veterans who were entitled to funds for attending college under the G.I. Bill of Rights, or who were eligible for disability compensation payments.

At first my assigned duties were mainly tabulating figures and writing awards throughout the business day. Numbers were always my forte, and it was not long before I was promoted to a supervisory position. I had lost my major arm, and here I was writing all day with my left arm only nine months after that day in July when I lay wondering if they would find me in time for a doctor to do me some good!

The basic problem I had to deal with during the first months at work was a personal one rather than anything to do with my work. In returning to civilian life, I had to convince myself that I could blend into the world of normal people again, that I could be accepted by them as an equal. I remember the summer days of 1945 when I was wearing a prosthesis with a mechanical hand covered by a brown glove. I used to try to conceal the fact that I wore an artificial arm by placing the left hand glove through the glove on the prosthesis, thereby making it look sporty. Slowly my confidence began to return. My almost immediate promotion helped quite a bit in making me realize that I could perform on a level equal to those who were not handicapped. This proof that I could do my job well encouraged me in other endeavors and quieted my early fears.

At about this time I joined the National Amputation Chapter

of the Disabled American Veterans, which is devoted to the care and welfare of all war amputees. I found this volunteer work very gratifying, and I began to concentrate most of my spare time on helping my fellow handicapped. This was outside my duties at the Veterans Administration, but my experience on the job was beginning to add up to a certain amount of know-how which enabled me to be of considerable help. I was able to secure benefits for amputee veterans from municipal and state governments and other benefits, such as insurance and medical care, which were not widely publicized at that time. I learned still more as I worked for the social rehabilitation of the wounded veteran. The labor and satisfaction of this volunteer work have increased in amount and in value to me. My spare time was continuously available to a vet in need. I served as historian of this organization and was elected commander in 1953. A unanimous vote for a second term as commander made me very proud and happy. Since the end of that term, I have been a permanent member of the Board of Directors.

As Chief of the Prosthetic and Sensory Aids Service, which is in the New York Regional Office, Medical Division, it is my job to counsel all disabled veterans on appliances best suited to their particular disabilities. Working in the name of the Veterans Administration, I contact manufacturers of appliances and devices and make arrangements to buy them for veterans who need them. I work from day to day with many categories of disability: I attempt to help solve the problems of the amputees, the blind, the deaf, and the paralyzed veterans. Men who require braces and other supports, special orthopedic shoes, various medical and surgical appliances and self-help devices (such as auto top invalid lifters, bathroom grab bars, special attachments for wheelchairs, oxygen equipment, etc.) come to my department by the thousands.

My confidence has increased. Through the years of working with handicapped people I have found a lot of the answers. When I am not able to come up with an answer or solution which seems right for a specific case, I consult associates in rehabilitation and, when my questions are answered, my store of knowledge is increased by that much. I think that I grow on my job. And then there are some unusual days, such as the time I appeared on television to promote National Employ the Physically Handicapped Week. The following day I was offered several jobs!

In 1946, I learned to drive a car, encountering no difficulty whatever since I used the special accessories prescribed for me by the State Motor Vehicle Bureau. These consisted of a wheel spinner, directional signals, and hand brake on the left to compensate for my right arm amputation. I like traveling and I have driven almost 150,000 miles since I got my license. Since driving is a "soother" to me, I vacation often by car, mostly in the East and Northeast.

I drive carefully when I am in my car, but I guess I drove a little too hard on the job when work increased steadily in volume, year after year. In November 1958, a cardiogram showed that I had suffered a heart attack. A long period of recuperation followed this diagnosis; I did not return to work until twenty weeks later. I have now been back on the job for ten months, pacing myself a little differently and remembering not to be disturbed by things which formerly upset me. I still make myself available to any and all callers who present problems on rehabilitation, and I still volunteer my services at the Veterans Organization.

My activities now are a little more limited. I can't play left field for the "Broken Wings" baseball team, which usually had no difficulty in beating the "Flat Tire" team of Amputee Veterans Organization, but then again I haven't played since 1952 when I "retired" to make way for a younger Korean War amputee. I still get off to a Broadway show every so often, go to baseball games, enjoy a good game of cards, and drive my car about 1,000 miles a month for simple enjoyment. I don't abuse myself and I stay within my fatigue limits. In the years to come I hope to be at my desk, ready to aid the thousands of friends I have made among wounded veterans and the many referrals I shall surely meet in the future.

Larry Giustino

Larry Giustino was born in Brooklyn in 1934 but he moved, while still a young child, to Kingston, N.Y. At thirteen, he began to study the piano, becoming proficient enough to give a number of public recitals. By seventeen, however, blindness as a result of Bechet's Syndrome set in. At present, Mr. Giustino is a patient in Goldwater Hospital in New York City.

I was going on seventeen when I began to feel bad in school one day. The doctor took my temperature and told me that I had a fever and should go home. I was glad of the chance to get out of school that day, but I sure never dreamed that I would not go back again.

I was in bed at home for a long time. My family was always real good to me. My grandmother and grandfather were living upstairs, and they were a lot of company for me. My father fixed up a television set so I could see the World Series from bed, and my mother was always there doing all she could to make the days easier.

But I got worse, and they sent me to Vassar Hospital in Poughkeepsie. My condition was diagnosed as rheumatic fever. I had swelling of the ankles and knees as well as fever. We had hospitalization with Mutual of Omaha, and we all thought that the expenses would be taken care of by them. But they were not, and my parents paid all they had, and then the money I had saved for college also had to be spent for hospital bills.

Then I was sent home for eight months of bed rest to prevent damage to my heart. I read medical books and Shakespeare. I liked *Romeo and Juliet*. Of course, I listened a lot to the opera, and I read about it. My aunt came over and said, "Now, Larry, you have to get well and out of that bed. I have a season ticket for the Met, and we'll go as soon as you can make it. What would you like to see?" I chose *Aida*. I love everything by Verdi. My grandfather's name is Giuseppe Verdi, and I've always wondered if the great Verdi could have been a relative of mine. I adore my family very much. My mother always knows and does the best thing for me.

I used to sketch scenes from the operas. Also I made a portrait of my mother and one of my sister and one of my father when he was eating with his mouth full.

Then my eyes began to act queer. When I moved my eyeballs, queer shapes moved with them. They looked like wild horses that moved whenever I moved my eyes. We called a doctor, and he told me to stay in bed. He did not understand my case and suggested that I might be taking too much medication. We called him a shoemaker.

My uncle, who is a cop in Brooklyn, came down one day, and when he saw me and realized how long I had been lying there in bed, he got furious. He insisted they take me to Beekman Street Hospital in New York, a place that was mainly for heart diseases. After a few months, the doctors at Beekman said there was nothing wrong with my heart but that the eye trouble was serious. They injected cortisone into my eyeballs. Finally they said, "Larry, the best thing is to go home and rehabilitate yourself."

So I went home and started a strawberry farm with my mother's help. I can tell you my mother is a real trooper. My family has a sincerity about life that I do not find in many people. After so long a time in a hospital I have learned to talk seriously with many different kinds of people and I think I understand them, but there is a special kind of sincerity in my own family which has helped me but which I cannot put into words.

I tried to go back to music. One night the doctor and his family came to hear me play. I tried a piece by Paderewski. To play it right you have to play it fast. I couldn't do it. I played slow. I couldn't keep time. I looked at my mother, and I could see that she knew how it was, that I *knew* how to play it but that my hands would not work as my brain wanted them to.

And when I walked, I could not walk straight either. My

mother got a little scared. I could tell she was worried. One day she tried to joke about it, "Larry, try to walk straight. People will think you have just come out of a bar."

Then they took me to Presbyterian Hospital at Columbia Medical Center. I heard one of the nurses say that I looked so bad they did not think I would last through the night. My mother stayed beside me. She loves me very much. And we fooled the doctors. I pulled through, but the next day my eyes were very bad, and my voice was so slow that it was hard for people to understand what I was trying to say. The cerebellum part of my brain was just not getting its messages through to my limbs or to my voice.

Now I feel that the more I walk, talk, etc., the easier it will be to do it. I can go get something; it takes longer, but I get there. But when I first went to Presbyterian Hospital, I couldn't do anything with my limbs or even talk well. Everyone said, "What, what?" They had to feed me. I used to wave the spoon so that by the time I found my mouth there wasn't anything on it.

The doctor said, "Larry, go home. There's nothing we can do. Go home and try to make the best of it." So I called my mother to bring my clothes. I told her to bring my best suit. She didn't understand anything I said. She said, "Yes, Larry, yes, Larry." Next day when she came she didn't bring it. She couldn't believe they were discharging me because she felt I wasn't well.

My uncle said he'd bring me a suit of clothes. He brought me one of his own suits, and I wore it home. I was home for a while. Then my eyes started to get worse. It was around Christmas time. I could just about see the Christmas tree. It looked beautiful. My mother was knitting, and I said, "Ma, what are you knitting?" I said, "Hey, Ma, you're getting fat." Then one day my grandmother told me that my mother was pregnant. I tell you I felt ten years younger. I felt so glad I wanted to run down the hall and yell. Sort of let the baby let my mother forget about me and put her mind on the baby instead of me. But that wasn't the case. She loved me even more.

My grandmother brought me a urinal. It was white. She brought it to my bed. That was the last thing I saw. White and a blue handle.

When I couldn't see, the world didn't come to an end. I could still talk and breathe. So then my mother said, "What are we going to do?" She called Presbyterian Hospital again, and they refused me. They recommended another hospital across the street, a neurological hospital. There is where the lady came to me with the Braille, and I said, "Who wants to learn *that*? I'm going to read again." But I learned it for curiosity's sake and thought if I took Braille I could maybe help other people. But now it's helping me.

So after a while I wanted to get up as much as possible. I felt good at times and bad at times. They said they couldn't do anything for me. So they sent me way up in the Bronx to Montefiore Hospital. But I felt I wasn't getting any better. So I called my mother and said, "Hey, Ma, come get me out of this cotton-picking hospital." I just wanted to get *out*. I thought I'd go home and rehabilitate myself. That was the main thing I needed.

Then I went to the Cerebral Palsy Hospital in Kingston. There I did exercises which helped me. So my mother got in touch with the American Foundation for the Blind. They got in touch with a teacher in Newburg, N.Y., who used to come to my house and tutor me in Braille. And now I was sincere about it. I felt there was a chance I wouldn't see again and would need it.

I learned fast. I passed the first grade Braille. The second grade was harder. Then third grade, which is the highest grade. If you can lick that you can read O.K. Braille is a very good sleeping pill for me. It's a funny thing—my eyes get very tired, and I want to go to sleep. I read a little bit every night. The more I read, the better I get.

My teacher graduated from New York State School for the Blind in Batavia. She recommended it, and I went there because of her. After the first year they got disgusted with me because I couldn't get around or talk well. I lived in a dormitory then. I learned to type at this school, and I learned to write Braille and to read better. Just before I was about to graduate, they approached me and said, "Larry, your studies are very poor. We'll have to send you home." And they were right. My studies were poor, but I went there for rehabilitation rather than studies. I had some music there, but I'd get disgusted with myself when I thought of how I used to play and all the concerts I'd played in. It made me feel discouraged to go on.

After I went home I wanted to rehabilitate myself, so I decided to go into business for myself. I started making belts. My mother helped me a great deal. I thought it would be best not to stay at home all the time, so I got in touch with a social worker who sent me to Buffalo Industrial School for the Blind. I was there one month. I tried working. I was living at a boarding house near Lake Erie. It was nice. But I was doing the work too slow because of my poor coordination. My work was accurate but not fast. They told me to come back in a couple of years if I was better. So I called my mother and said I wanted to go home. I used to travel on the train by myself; people put me on and took me off. That's the way I travel now.

When I got home I wanted to do something with my life, so I went back to making belts. My mother got orders for me. I got a lot of orders. I used to get up and be at my workshop at 8:00 A.M. I listened to the radio at the same time. I had an hour for lunch, and at 1:00 on the button I went back to work and worked 'til 4:30. I used to average about eight belts a day. The money I made I put in the bank. I had a good profit. So I said to myself, "I'm going to buy my mother something she needs." So I ordered an automatic clothes dryer. I got it all worked out with my grandmother. My friend was at the house that day. I said, "Mom, when the truck comes I want you to go upstairs." It was Christmas. I made him tie a big red ribbon on it. She came down, and she almost fainted away. She felt so good, and I felt so good. I like to play Santa Claus with someone else on *my* money, not what's given to me by charity. So I used up all the profit I had made on my belts. My mother had helped me so much, and I wanted to do something for her. I really enjoyed it. Even my friend had tears in his eyes. Money you make with your own hands and give away makes you feel wonderful. When I felt her face I wanted to cry. But you know men don't cry.

I was home for a while, and then a friend said he knew a good hospital in New York. And through friends I went to live in Brooklyn for a while with my grandparents. Then my grandmother died and I could no longer live there. We got a doctor who recommended this hospital, where I am now. I've been here four years, and I love this place because it keeps me very busy.

My religion had failed me a great deal before I came to this hospital. One day I was near the chapel at the hospital, so I went in. Then I started to go twice a week, then three times. Then they moved me to another building. I met a friend, and he gave me instruction. He's a sincere guy with a warm heart. When things go in one ear I think about them and turn them over before they come out. But when he talked to me it stayed in.

When I went to the shrine of St. Ann in Canada, I asked for a physical miracle but said if she couldn't do that would she give me grace and peace in my heart. St. Ann did that. From then on in the hospital I went to the chapel every day. Then I went three or four times a day. I have to go down three flights and go about five blocks now to get to the chapel. I receive communion every day, and afterward I feel good on the inside.

Now I have the courage to go to other parts of the hospital and visit other people. I'm kept busy all day long since I've gotten to be very sociable. Now that I can express myself better, I want to know more people. I have a typewriter, and I hope it will help me increase my contacts with people outside the hospital. I also have a little portable radio. In the evenings I often enjoy listening to news and music and smoking my pipe on the porch outside my ward.

Have you ever noticed how blind people look up? I figure if you're completely blind like me, you have the kinesthetic sense more developed. The blank wall looms up before you very black. Sometimes even when there's no one in the hall my voice bounces back. You can see by the way the air moves. And people say, "Oh, Larry, you're a big faker making people think you're blind."

Life in the hospital—it's according to what hospital you're in. They show movies in my ward, but they're mostly very old, back in the thirties. You know, the second-grade film starring somebody you never heard of. Well, that's what they show us. I don't like westerns. Often other people are so busy looking they don't always remember to tell you about the movie. When you see westerns, all you hear is bang, bang, and people running away on horses, and you don't know what happens. Not much of a plot, just bang, bang. But I like to listen to variety shows with comedy or regular dramas on television when they're loud and when there's not more than three or four characters. You can study the voices and know who's talking.

A couple of my best friends died, one of diabetes and one of spinal arthritis. One friend who instructs me about my religion is an amputee. I meet this friend, Joe Enright, by the chapel every day. He's always got that minute to talk to me. He's so very busy, takes part in a lot of activities, but he's always got time to take a minute out and talk. We sit and smoke together, and he tells me everything I would like to know about the mass or the saints. I went to the shrine in Canada with him, and I was with him all the time—well, not all of the time because I was a nuisance trying to get around.

I like people. I feel that I want to meet as many people as I can, just to talk to them. I like to get with people more now than when I could see. I get to know the person by touch, by his manner of speech. They say it's remarkable, but I myself know that I make many mistakes. Sometimes it's hard to come out with your impression of people when you first see them. It takes time to figure out things.

Sometimes I'm lonely, but even on days when I don't feel well I do the exercises that I hope are slowly teaching the cerebellum part of my brain to transmit its messages better to my hands and legs and voice. I am better now than I was, but the progress is slow and discouraging sometimes. But I believe you can get results in this illness if you really keep at it, trying to help yourself get well.

Dorothy Pallas   Dorothy Pallas was born in Moonachie, N.J. in 1931, and, except for time spent in a number of hospitals, she has lived there ever since. When she was seven years old, she was stricken with polio. Her schooling was completed in hospitals and at home, and she was graduated *summa cum laude* from Fairleigh Dickinson University in 1953 under a special arrangement whereby she studied at home. She has since collaborated with Dr. Carroll Lane Fenton on four books about nature. Miss Pallas is also a published poet. She lives in a specially equipped room in her family home.

I was seven years old and in the midst of a busy summer when I became ill. During Dad's vacation we were taking day-trips to the World's Fair, Coney Island, the lake at Green Valley Park, Lake Parsippany. . . . It was fun. Then one day I had chills and didn't want any ice cream. My aunt wrapped her son's baby blanket around my shoulders. We went home from our visit early. The next day I had a frightful headache and a fever. After a visit to the doctor I was put to bed. The next morning when I got out of bed, my legs folded under me. The doctor thought it was infantile paralysis.

A few days later I was in a respirator at Bergen Pines Hospital hearing the doctors describe the course of the disease, which had reached my neck and was expected shortly to be fatal. I was being fed intravenously. I couldn't move a muscle from my chin downward, couldn't swallow or turn my head, though I did keep talking and discovered I could wriggle my ears.

Despite the prognosis, the crisis passed and some functions returned quickly. In a few months' time I was breathing, digesting, and swallowing, and had some motion in my hands and arms.

Since then the muscles that returned have gained strength and I've learned to use them in many new ways, but I doubt that any important additional recovery from the original paralysis has taken place.

A great and lasting change seems, when viewed from a little distance, to break life into two, bringing what *was* to an end and leaving what *will be* in the dark. But as I lived through the great change of paralysis, I felt no break at all. For one thing, I still thought and reacted as I did before my illness. It was years before I admitted and understood that this was I, Dorothy Pallas, paralyzed for good, and by that time many of the new ways had already become habits so there was little shock to my awakening. Furthermore, when my new life took shape, it wasn't really so new after all. In most important respects it was woven of threads from the past.

Before polio I was as happy a child in as happy a place as I've ever heard of. I read *The Bobbsey Twins*; I caught polywogs and killies in the muddy Moonachie ditches; I climbed trees and did acrobatics on the swing and bar in our large back yard. Flowers, birds, baseball, and hopscotch were also a great part of life. I read more than most children of seven, and I enjoyed school. For my seventh birthday Mother gave me a book of poems by Robert Louis Stevenson. I promptly read it from beginning to end and added the author to my constantly shifting list of boy friends.

During my illness Miss Bell, the private nurse, read to me. Through the fever, then through the lengthening hours out of the lung, through the first days breathing entirely on my own, and through the first experiments with moving again, she read to me. Afterward I read to myself, even though that meant hailing someone to come and turn each page. In self-defense Mother helped find a position in which to place the bed table, the book, and my left hand so I could turn a page or two with the back of my thumb and some stomach jiggling. Later, I discovered how to hold a book against my left arm and turn pages with the tips of my fingers. Reading has since been a strong thread from the old life, worked unbroken into the new.

For the first seven years post-polio, I spent many months in many hospitals. Some time during that period, without knowing it, I made a decision. I could not put all my energy into getting well. I wanted too much to live and do things, whether or not I moved again. I knew some patients who learned to take a few struggling steps using braces and crutches and never got any further. I saw the tremendous energy that this required, and I wondered where so few steps could take them.

Perhaps the thing that held me back from thinking such thoughts openly was fear of being called a quitter and a coward, the one who couldn't take it. I was accused of that as it was. I screamed during back-bending and heel-stretching, a disgrace to my braver companions, the ones with "grit." Or perhaps the reason I kept these thoughts from my conscious mind was the fact that I didn't really think of myself as paralyzed until years later. At any rate, I know now that, rightly or wrongly, I divided my strength between treatments, sawing away at the prison bars, and making do—painting the prison walls and hanging pictures.

At home, between hospital stays, I spent much time outdoors. From the windows of the dining room in which my hospital bed was placed I could also watch the gardens and woods. My earlier interest in pollywogs, birds, and anything that moved, became channeled to bird-watching. Birds came to the tree outside my window. I didn't need to move to see them and enjoy them. Bird-watching and reading about birds eventually led to bird writing. I've had books and poems published which are the result of this second strong thread from the past.

Schooling was provided for me at home and in hospitals. The New Jersey Rehabilitation Commission paid the expenses of college instruction, which also came to me at home through Fairleigh Dickinson University. During college I was encouraged in my bird study and writing. I also met the president of the New Jersey Audubon Society, who was confident that I could write about birds and introduced me to Dr. Carroll Lane Fenton, author of many children's nature books. Soon Dr. Fenton and I were collaborating on *Birds and Their World*. Since then we have written four other books.

I have no illusions about my writing "success." I take full

credit for it because I have put effort, whatever talent I possess, and initiative into it. But still it is entirely dependent. Without assistance at every turn, the mere mechanics of writing would be impossible. My family has helped in some extraordinary ways, from catching grasshoppers to feed to a baby sparrow hawk to equipping a station wagon for a trip to Florida. My parents and my sisters, Amy and Hazel, have filled bird feeders, "watched" turtles, and pushed, carried, and dragged my stretcher through sand, brush, briers, and mud—not always with the best of humor but nevertheless well. More to the point is the endless round of "Put up the table. Hand me the pen. Bring me the book. Pick up what I dropped. Take away the book. Can you type now, Mother?"

I am fortunate in having people around me who are willing to do extras. What would happen if I didn't? I hope I would concentrate on things which wouldn't involve so much help. A very important part of my present life is studying the Bible and sharing what I learn with others. I am one of Jehovah's Witnesses. With a minimum of help from people, I know I can go on increasing in knowledge of God and growing in faith. So long as I have a window, I know I can also go on enjoying birds, seasons, and weather.

However, it isn't a decrease in assistance that is likely to curtail my activities but increase of disability. Recent illnesses have made breathing difficult, so that I cannot speak well enough to dictate. My left arm has been weakened, so that writing is slow and wearing. If there is not much improvement, writing books will be out of the question. But my disabilities are circumstances of my life which I must accept in order to enjoy the goodness there is in all life. Life is so wonderful and so completely undeserved that I have no wish to complain of having less of it than someone else. If a great deal of it is desirable, then even a small amount is something to be prized.

To the severely handicapped, existence itself depends upon constant care. Sometimes we wonder if it is fair to impose this care on the people who happen to be near, family and friends. I have thought about this often and believe that just as our disabilities are circumstances of life which must be accepted if unchangeable, so the duty of caring for us is a circumstance of life to those on whom it falls. We should appreciate their help and give thanks for it but never waste our strength worrying about its fairness.

In poetry, for my own sake, I have tried to apologize for those of us who feel less than brave, less than inspired. My latest attempt reads:

> *Bravery we do not need,*
> *Lack of fear, heroic deed,*
> *But courage that can take*
> *A shattered world and from it make*
> *Meanings entire,*
> *Courage that can glean*
> *Where pain has picked bones clean*
> *And feed an inner fire.*

Some day I hope to say it better.

Harold Nachmanson

Harold Nachmanson was born in Brooklyn on December 24, 1920. Prior to entering the armed forces in 1944, he worked at a variety of jobs. After the war, Mr. Nachmanson returned to his education and earned a B.A. degree from the City College of New York. He studied also at Long Island University and at New York University. At present, Mr. Nachmanson is taking his M.A. in Rehabilitation Counseling at Hunter College. A member of the Blind Veterans Association and the Jewish War Veterans, he enjoys traveling to places of historic interest, boating, and tutoring. Mr. Nachmanson plans to be married shortly.

I did not begin to lose my vision until I was about twenty-two. It began to fail slowly; for the first few years I experienced a gradual, progressive loss, but during the five years after that my remaining vision was lost rapidly. One goes blind alone, as alone as one is born and as alone as one dies. I cannot see the experience except as an intensely inner crisis. Expectations that family and friends and people in general will understand it end in disappointment, and efforts at explanation, no matter how natural and how detailed and earnest, result, at best, in *partial* understanding which is often quickly lost.

Perhaps the fact that I lost my vision in middle age places me in a better position than many other people to discuss the problems which, though common to both sighted and blind, are nevertheless different for a person without vision—different and harder.

I think the problem of authority, the need for it in early years and the need to reject some of it as one grows up, is common to everyone. When I was a boy, my mother was the person whom I respected most. My father, too, depended on her for initiative.

Our family was large, and we did not have much money. As a result, both my parents worked. My mother made all the arrangements for establishing credit, finding a good location for a store, and purchasing merchandise to sell. Yet her children never felt a lack of love or care or attention. Quite objectively now, I can say that my first "authority figure" *deserved* my admiration.

When I was sixteen, I began to go to school at night and to work full time during the days. I began to mature beyond the need for my mother's advice and to feel some enjoyable independence, but I guess the problem of accepting (or not accepting) authority stays with most boys a long time. When I was eighteen, I went to work for my oldest brother, who owned a furniture business. *His* authority over me was not easy to accept. It extended too quickly and too often to personal matters as well as to the daily business details which, of course, he had a right to manage. I left my brother's business and got a job where I was not personally dominated and was decently paid for my work.

When I lost my vision in 1955, I needed both advice and money, but I did not know where to turn for either. I finally got in touch with the New York State Commission for the Blind in New York City. One of the counselors gave me all the time I needed to discuss money problems, my personal values, the things which blocked me, and the things I wanted to do. He saw to it that I had medical care and psychological examinations to help me determine what steps I should take in what direction. He guided me through a tempestuous sea of doubt, fear, and insecurity. One never forgets a debt like this, a debt to a person who was *really there* every time I needed to talk to him.

But by this time I was mature, and I had learned that all people in authority are by no measure capable of using it wisely or well. The blind are particularly at the mercy of ignorant or malevolent people; eyes are a great help in determining whom to trust and respect.

At a state meeting of the New York Commission for the Blind, the same organization which had helped me immeasurably, I heard a commission member say, "Secretaries do the work of the blind executive." This, of course, made me angry, but I am glad that I

was old enough to be able to enumerate a number of sighted executives who play golf or have lunch all day while their secretaries
get the business done. And central in my thoughts were a few
blind executives who could not be more responsible than they are
about all the details of their work. It certainly is the rule, not the
exception, that they work harder than sighted men in similar positions, having to commit to memory what the sighted keep in files,
and having to use double-checking care and thought and judgment
again and again instead of visual, off-the-cuff, impressions.

Although I know that radio and television have worked with
this idea to some extent, I often dream of a radio, or preferably
a television network which would devote a full one- or two-hour
weekly program to the complete externalization of the problems of
handicapped persons. Short programs do not accomplish even a
fraction of what a fully developed life-drama could achieve in the
way of clarification and information and understanding. It takes
time to learn about people who are different from the average. A
person who sees a short program about a man in a wheelchair and
then thinks he knows the answers is like Billy Graham going to
India and coming back with the idea that sending Nehru a gold
Buick will fix up our international relationships. It's not that easy.

If my dream about these programs ever comes true, the separate dramas will not be success stories but ordinary life situations
that present the truth about disability rather than the sensational
or incredible career. And all the aspects of the problem should be
portrayed, not just learning to walk or to lip-read or to read Braille,
but also having dinner with a friend, falling in love, shopping for
a record or a book, doing things for other people, taking a bath or
a vacation or a subway ride, trying to get a job or to get registered
in school.

Because of their frequent rejection by employers and by schools,
it is only natural that many of the blind feel inadequate and inferior. I have been turned away from many jobs I could do. I
have had my share of experience in managing personnel. I was a
railroad supervisor for the Erie Railroad for several years, and the
men I supervised came out of the Bowery and the slum districts

of Chicago. Their work consisted of the replacement of ties, steel tracks, gravel beds, and the relocation of wrecked boxcars. Almost without exception their pleasure consisted of getting very drunk. Supervising them was not easy, and it often called for imagination and strength, but it was a job from which I learned, pretty well, I think, what I could do and could not do in a supervisory capacity. Yet I have been turned away more often than I like to remember from jobs I could handle with my eyes closed, so to speak, and my hands tied behind my back as well.

Handicapped people are not only turned away from jobs they can do well, but it is common experience for them to be turned away from schools and colleges by registrars or advisers who do not even take the trouble to find out that they sometimes have scores in scholastic aptitude and their own ways of taking notes and getting reading materials and being valuable to the schools.

In the years since I have been blind, I have received help in a few very important respects, for which I am deeply grateful; I have also learned enough about the general situation of the handi- capped to be very indignant about other things.

My indignation rises from many minor but inescapable inci- dents which, on discouraging days, seem everywhere to be part of the "American way of life." It is downright confusing to me when people say, as they often do, "You *must* be able to see because you turn your face to us." Perhaps when I have finished school and am at last doing the work I am preparing to do, I shall have time to practice turning my back to people when they speak to me. When a person loses vision in middle age, many of his established habits and manners remain as they were. This fact eases many a social situation, keeping the blind person from needing any special attention or concern. But, quite characteristically, the blind get blamed for their accomplishments and for anything they do which is normal and efficient. It simply isn't pleasant to be called a fake when you are blind and have discovered a few ways not to be a nuisance about it.

This is only one example, but a typical one, of what causes per- sonal annoyance. Of much greater importance are things I have observed of organized attitudes toward the handicapped. Certain agencies for the help of the handicapped get money from the government for sheltered workshop programs and other forms of direct, personal dole. Even if I did not have other reasons for believing that a long list of dependent sightless people is an advantage to an agency for the blind, logic itself would lead me to think that, under these circumstances, little effort is expended to help the blind person toward independence and self-respect and his rightful share of pride and happiness.

I believe that, with *any* handicap, it is most vital that a person develop, to a point normal people never have to, the faculty of choice-making. Not many choices are *given* to us; we must learn to make our own as realistically and honestly as we can and then find the way to prepare for making our lives what we want them to be. I don't think any agency or any welfare worker, no matter how well-intentioned, can do this as well as the individual himself.

Secondly, I believe that more blind people should do the work for the blind. Public ignorance is a Grand Canyon it would take too long to fill up. We should simply set about *doing*—singly, in small groups, in large ones, making use of what we know and the public does not know, to help the handicapped use their full resources and live richer and better lives.

The making of my own choices was sometimes painful and difficult. The plan of action which followed decision seemed at times to be blocked in every direction. Now I am near the attainment of what I long ago decided was the most important thing in my life. I am now almost fully prepared to teach and promote the welfare of mentally retarded or underprivileged children. For such children physical health, emotional support and affection, and education at the proper level should be considered together, not separately, as they often are at the present time. I want to be good at this work; it seems to me a whole lot more important than the Erie Railroad. Being really good at it will probably require about two years "in the field," working with children so that I can learn the feel of it and can add practical knowledge to what I have learned in school.

I'm not sure exactly why, but when I think of the work that I am at last almost ready to begin, I think of a little Polish boy who used to live in my neighborhood in Brooklyn. I think of him as being ten years old forever. Without love or care or encouragement, he was a "bad boy." He broke windows and a lot of other things. Ideally, I shall find a way to work in a nonsectarian, interracial organization which will give me the freedom to make happy men out of such little boys as this one I so fondly remember.

I am sure that I have not incurred much malice. But what I have met is much worse: ignorance and indifference which keep me on a treadmill. I happen to feel— even to know—that I am capable of doing work which is much more meaningful, much more remunerative, and, above all, much more in line with what I am and what I can do.

CHARLES ROBERTS

CHAPTER **3**

Education and Afterward

The contributions included in this chapter center around education and work, two aspects of the life of a handicapped individual which are usually classified under the heading Vocational Rehabilitation. The problems discussed here are by no means peculiar to the handicapped person. The desire for education, along with the desire to improve one's economic and occupational status, are closely linked to the American cultural ethos—a problem about which we shall have more to say in the Postscript.

And yet, as our contributors so effectively point out, in his quest for an education and a suitable occupation, the handicapped individual is the victim of certain public stereotypes. Blind people, for example, are somehow expected to find fulfillment in making brooms or in operating transcribing machines. But some blind people, having been born with a certain kind of intelligence or with a certain kind of sensitivity, are simply not happy making brooms or operating transcribing machines. Charles Roberts is among those of our contributors who have mastered the educational hurdle with little apparent difficulty, and yet, despite his brilliant academic record, he is employed as a government typist; despite his having passed difficult governmental examinations with high grades, despite his having been recommended for promotion, he finds that he is looked upon as simply a *blind* man, a fact that is supposed to make him "grateful to have work at all." And the federal government is probably far more liberal than most private businesses in its employment policy toward handicapped individuals.

The special problems that the handicapped individual must face in order to acquire an education, especially a college education, are also dealt with here. Some handicapped people, like Melvin Schoonover, are taking great physical risk merely in seeking an education; others, like Richard Moore, find themselves discouraged from pursuing a particular goal for reasons which seem to have nothing to do with their handicaps. While still a graduate student at Michigan State University, Dr. Moore was told by one of his professors, "My students have to dissect frogs in zoology, but they do not have to accept you as a teacher." Now a professor of biology at Hardin-Simmons University, Dr. Moore does not seem to have suffered unduly from this remark. But other handicapped individuals, confronted with similar statements, might well have quit the academic world in discouragement.

On the whole, the eight contributors to this chapter are "successful" individuals: six of them have completed college, one is still in college, and the other is soon to enter college. All six of those who have completed college have continued studying for advanced degrees—certainly an exceptional record. But all of them have paid a great deal for their success. For the handicapped individual is constantly being called upon to prove himself, only to find, after each new success, that he must prove himself again.

John DeWitt McKee was born in Emporia, Kan., on December 22, 1919, a victim of cerebral palsy. Between the ages of five and seventeen he underwent five operations but managed to complete his high school

John DeWitt McKee

education. After he received his B.A. from Kansas Wesleyan University in 1943, Mr. McKee worked as a newspaper reporter, sports editor, editorial columnist, and house-organ editor. Returning to the academic world, he received his M.A. in English literature in 1952 and his Ph.D. in American studies in 1959, both from the University of New Mexico. As a graduate student, he supported himself by teaching and free-lance writing. His book, *Two Legs to Stand On*, was published by Appleton-Century-Crofts in 1955. He is married and is now an assistant professor of Humanities at New Mexico Institute of Mining and Technology.

There are clichés about disability, handicap, misfortune, affliction, and sorrow of all kinds that have bothered me ever since I have been old enough to think about them. One of these is the picture of the ever-cheerful cripple, typified for all time by Charles Dickens' Tiny Tim. If I'm any criterion, the answer to this view of disability may be borrowed from the American commander at the Battle of the Bulge: "Nuts!"

I was born a little over forty years ago, and I came into the world two months prematurely. I brought with me a condition that was to make me even more different from the rest of the human race than one person is normally different from all others. I was born with cerebral palsy.

That means that either before, during, or immediately following my birth, I suffered an injury to the motor nerve centers of my brain. That injury resulted in spastic paralysis of both my legs and of my right arm, though miraculously my speech was spared. The circumstance of my birth meant that I did not walk until I was six years old, and then only after surgery. It meant that my mother had to pull me to school in a coaster wagon for my first year so that I could start my education at the proper age. It meant that I had to undergo surgery four more times before I was seventeen, and that I would have to relearn walking after each operation.

I cannot say I was always cheerful about it. By the time the fifth operation loomed, I did not look forward to the pre-operational catharsis, to the shaving of my legs and pubic zone, to lying all night in wet bichloride bandages before the operation, or to the weeks of immobility in plaster casts that followed the operation. I resisted the agonizing and fearful necessity of learning to walk again. Sometimes I found the passive exercises at which my mother assisted a painful bore and a subtraction from the time I could have been outside playing with my brothers. In other words, I was a normal boy—cheerful or moody, biddable or rebellious, active and gregarious or contemplative and solitary—within the physical limits of that normality.

When Will Shakespeare murmurs in my inner ear, "Sweet are the uses of adversity," my inner voice is likely to retort, "Speak for yourself, Will." There is nothing sweet about being past forty and still doing exercises in physical therapy to improve my balance and to correct a gait that has more than once been ascribed to drunkenness. There is nothing sweet in feeling good about the gait and suddenly catching sight of my lurching reflection in the window of a store or seeing my shadow bobbing grotesquely before me. Still, if the uses of adversity are not sweet, they *are* uses.

It is possible that if I had had all my physical faculties, I would not have concentrated on scholastic achievement. I was the first of my family to get a college education. This involved much sacrifice on the part of my parents who sent me away from home, for the first time in my life, to solve my own problems of getting around, of living with other people, and of taking responsibility for my own life. In college I began to develop a certain talent for writing and paid part of my way through school working in public relations and editing the school newspaper. In the summers when I was going to school, I worked on the weekly newspapers in the small towns where we lived in Kansas.

I could not have done this, or anything else that I did then or was to do, had it not been for my family. My father and mother and my two brothers took me as I was. I was not someone to be treated specially. Above all, I was not hothoused in sentimental sympathy. I played grade school baseball and football and lost a front tooth because I forgot to duck in a boxing match with my brother Ellwood.

Because they emphasized my abilities rather than my disabilities, my family were as much responsible for my eventual mobility as were the doctors, nurses, and therapists who did the cutting, stretching, and tending. But the most important gift my family ever gave me was the ability, and the willingness, to live *as a person* among people, and the unastonished knowledge that I could do so. Indeed, it is only at times like this, when I strip myself and stand before the mirror of self-analysis, that I become acutely conscious that the world outside myself considers me handicapped.

For though I am more visibly, more tangibly handicapped than most, I do not consider myself more handicapped than many. I with my spastically tense legs, I with the T-strap brace on my left leg, I with only the index finger of my spastic right hand helping my uninvolved left hand punch out these words on the typewriter —I am no more handicapped than you with your psychosomatic ulcer, you with your frustrated passion for power, you with your abject and quivering fear of the mushroom cloud that is the *memento mori* of our age.

So, Will Shakespeare, I owe you at least a half-apology. For adversity creates the maze that leads from what we cannot do to what we can. After I was graduated from college, I worked on daily newspapers, wrote sports publicity, and edited a magazine at the University of New Mexico; but I never made enough money to live alone. I went with the family when the family moved. Always I was sharpening my writing tools—a poem published here, an article there, a short story somewhere else. But always, too, I was conscious that the jobs I had were dead-end jobs. I knew by then that I was not physically fast enough for sustained daily newspaper work. I knew by then, too, that, much as I loved sports, there had to be more in life for me than climbing to the pressbox on Saturdays and chronicling the seasons by the size and shape of the ball in use. So, to borrow from E. B. White, what I took to be a door turned out to be a painted decoy again, and again I bumped my nose.

After one of those capricious economy waves broke and took me out with the tide, I stayed at home and tried free-lance writing for about six months. It was like betting on the horses using pants buttons for money, and when my father offered to stake me to a year in which to get my master's degree—the idea being that I should then go into high school teaching—I accepted.

Not that I wanted to teach. I had always felt more comfortable in front of a typewriter than behind a lectern, but I was tired of the dead ends. So I went back to the university as a student, and I earned a Master's degree in English literature. In the process, I wrote one of the three theses produced that year under the just-inaugurated program in creative writing. That thesis, *Two Legs to Stand On*, was finally licked and whittled into a book and published in 1955. Perhaps if it had not been for the dead-end jobs and the too-early leap into freelancing, if I had not had to produce a thesis for a degree, I would not have written my first book.

Meantime, more because I was exasperated by the idea that I could not do it than for any other reason, I learned to swim, finally, in 1948. Because we had moved to the country and to take a bus to work meant getting up in the dark hours when sleep is sweetest, I learned to drive a car in 1949. None of this was easy, and the frustration attendant on keeping leaden legs afloat and on achieving the intricate coordination necessary to shift gears was sweet as vinegar.

In the process of getting my Master's degree I discovered that, in order to teach in the high schools of New Mexico, I would have to take a number of courses in education. The maze again. I dutifully enrolled in one course, survived the semester, and swore off. There weren't even any withdrawal pains. Because of my aversion to such nonsense as "The Philosophy of Education," "The History of Education," and "The Theory of Education," I stayed in graduate school, determined to get the Ph.D. and teach at the college level. With the aid of a fellowship and assistantships, and through doing free-lance and part-time news jobs, I made it. Now I'm teaching English in a technical institute and have at least some time to prove to myself whether or not I'm a writer. Such have been my uses of adversity.

And yet I will go with Shakespeare further than with the perpetrators of that nonsense about pain ennobling the spirit. Pain itself ennobles nothing. It is a grasping hand that strips away the mask of flesh and shows the spirit, whether it be noble or niggardly, a fighter or a coward. Pain tempers the metal, perhaps, but the metal must be there. I have been carried in this flat-wheeled coach of flesh so long, been so overly conscious of it, had it in the repair shop so often, that by now pain is a familiar companion with me in the carriage. And I do not find him pleasant company, much less ennobling.

Mortify the flesh, perhaps, and exalt the spirit. But pain does not stop with the flesh. When I was in my thirties, I went to work; I went to school; I was a member of numerous organizations; I had a warm place in the midst of my family; I was surrounded by people all my waking hours—and I was lonely unto death. For I went to bed alone, and I got up alone, and in my future I could not see it otherwise.

For what woman would be so foolish and so brave as to take into her heart the half-man that I thought I was? This was the greatest pain, not the loneliness of now, but the practical assurance of loneliness forever. The post-surgery breath and stink of ether, the jumping of the legs inside the casts, the anguish of the recurring first steps, the falls with their bumps, bruises, cuts, and battered dignity were as nothing compared to the pain of the loneliness.

Then, when I had quite given up looking, or even hoping, there she was, just such a divinely foolish, brave one as I had believed I would not find. She made me see that I was failing in my own precepts, that loneliness for me was a self-imposed pain. Now we are together, and that pain is gone.

It did not ennoble me, that pain. It oozed me imperceptibly into hateful resignation and the comfortable discomfort of self-pity.

What now? I think I have found my way out of the maze—that particular maze, at any rate. I have searched for a place in the world, and I have found one. I am a teacher, and despite doubts and frustrations, despite self-castigation and an occasional pulling at the halter of academic inanity, I know that I am doing something I *can* do. I am a writer, and maybe, by the time I'm eighty, like Bronson Alcott, I shall feel that I have served my apprenticeship. Thanks to many men and women—my father, my mother, my brothers, my wife, doctors, nurses, therapists, teachers, and employers—I am my own man.

I walk into the future who should have crawled or let the future come to me. I help others shape their lives and might myself have been a passive lump for others' shaping. I, who might have had to spend my life only in taking, can now give. My handicap? Well, if that is what you call it, it's still here. But it's like the briefcase that I carry in my work; I'd feel undressed without it.

Carol David
Carol David was born a cerebral palsy victim in Louisville, Ky., in 1942. When she was fourteen years old, her parents moved to Stamford, Conn., where Miss David is now attending high school. She looks forward to a college career.

I want to go to college. I've been looking forward to college for quite some time, and I'm excited at the prospect of going next fall. I'll be taking the college board exams this year, and I hope I do well in them. I wish I had some way of knowing which colleges would be willing to accept students with handicaps like mine. I have several catalogues and have been reading them from cover to cover, but I can't find out from the catalogues whether or not a good grade on the college board exams will be enough to admit me.

I know now which colleges I think I would like, but I surely wish I could tell which ones would like me. I think I'd like to go to a woman's college because I don't like the idea of competing with men in my college work. Of course, this doesn't mean I don't like men but, rather, that I do like them and don't want to be put in competition against them. And anyway I like to be with women. I think it's fun to be with girls my own age. I really don't know what I want to be yet, but library work interests me. I like literature, and I like history. I think I'd like to go to a liberal arts college, a good liberal woman's college.

I like reading. I think I really get more pleasure from reading than from anything else. And I like to listen to records, classical, calypso—I'm especially fond of calypso—and scores from musical shows. I saw *My Fair Lady*. It was great. And I like dramas and comedies, especially *Play of the Week* on television, but I don't watch television very much because most of my evening time goes into studying. Of the westerns on television I like *The Deputy* and *Gunsmoke.* I like disk jockeys and church music, but I'm not fond of jazz or any of the beatnik stuff. I hate beatnik stuff and hillbilly music—Oh, I *hate* it. It bores me to study the technicalities of music, but I enjoy listening to it.

I don't have any particular friend, but I do have some friends who are nice. Occasionally we go to movies together. I just don't have a particular friend I can talk with whenever I want to. I don't know many people with cerebral palsy—I know only one girl who has it. She doesn't have it bad, though. She's right-handed, and she gets along very well. Her speech is fairly normal.

When I started to school, and even for quite a long time afterward, I didn't realize that I was in any way different from other children. I entered the first grade at St. Francis of Assisi in Louisville and went there four years. Then my family moved to Jeffersontown, a rural community outside Louisville, where I went to school for three years. The school at Jeffersontown was quite primitive. We even had double desks, and because we were so crowded I didn't get much out of those three years. Then we moved back to Louisville, where we had a big white house and a big yard full of beautiful big trees. I loved to walk in the yard because it was almost like a park. I went to school at St. Raphael's and then to a Catholic high school. When I was fourteen we came to Stamford, and I started attending junior high school, which I liked very much. I liked the idea of being with all kinds of boys and girls. Then I came to Stamford High, which, in comparison with the other schools, seemed somewhat big to me, but I enjoyed it anyway.

I like public schools better than parochial schools, but I think you can get a good education in any school if your attitude is that of a student. When I entered public school I already had a good background. Everybody with like aptitudes was put in the same class, and I think that when students of like aptitudes are in class together, the interest level is much higher. In parochial school there was only one curriculum. I think religion should be kept out of schools, but I truly think religion is important. It doesn't play a very important part in my life; I was never very religious, but I do believe in the Gospel.

During the time that I was in the first and second grades I became aware that I was having trouble with my speech. Then I became interested in grammar. I think grammar has been worked out to fulfill a purpose, and I try to use good grammar in order that I may express my ideas as clearly as possible. I like language, and I think English is a *great* language. I'm interested in reading good books, I've studied Willa Cather and Dickens. I like *Gone With the Wind*, and most especially I like *The Mill on the Floss*. I thought it was so tender and brought out the emotions of the characters so well. The leading male character, Philip, is so well done. I felt for him because I know someone like Philip. He went to school with me. I also like *Wuthering Heights*, which I'm re-reading now. I always get more out of a book on rereading. I like Heathcliff, but I detest Cathy. Heathcliff does a lot of bad things, but you can understand him.

I've read Kenneth David's biography of Adlai Stevenson, and that was quite nice. I like Adlai Stevenson very much. I'd *love* to meet him. I think he's a man of ideas, a good leader. He's what our country needs. His language is beautiful. I always listen carefully when he speaks on the radio or television because I enjoy the skill with which he uses words. I've also read Kenneth David's biography of Eisenhower. I like Eisenhower, but I'm not particular about him. I think he's doing a good job. I *do* hope I can meet Stevenson.

I wish I were as skillful in using the English language as Stevenson is. I think I'd like to write. I've written a few things but nothing worth remarking about. I did a quite lengthy report on *All the King's Men*, by Robert Penn Warren. It hasn't been graded yet, but I liked it. In college I hope I can meet other people who are interested in writing so that we can talk together about it.

I enjoy going to school because I want to develop my mind. I don't care for Latin but I like modern languages, especially French. I take economics because I think it's practical for everyone to understand business. A very nice lady drives me to school every day, but I walk to our public library; I like the library very much.

I also go shopping, and I like to pick out things for myself. My mother has very good taste, but I like to make my own choices. I think it's important for people like me to be as independent as they can. I haven't gone into New York City by myself, though. I'd be afraid of people pushing in Grand Central Station.

Once during a show put on by our school I shared a dressing room with Rosemary Clooney. I'd never heard of her before, and I wasn't much impressed by her. But one thing in particular happened. I remember, I touched her shoe. I don't know why. It was a silver shoe, and I just remember touching it lying on the couch.

I like to travel. We've been around the East, and I've enjoyed it. I've been in all of the states east of the Mississippi. I like Massachusetts and Pennsylvania; I think Pennsylvania is a beautiful state. But for living I like Connecticut, not only because it's beautiful but because it's near New York. It's been hard on my parents traveling with all us kids, but I've appreciated the opportunity to travel about as other people do.

I believe handicapped people should be allowed to do the things they can do. They should be treated as individuals. I think it's a crime to make handicapped people weave baskets or make potholders just because they *are* handicapped. I want to use my mind. At the testing center where I go I've been given little things to screw together as a part of a test. I hate working with little things, and I don't want to be put to work at something silly. I hope they won't do that to me. Sewing or anything like that is so boring that I can't stand it. I don't have any patience with work of that kind, but I like using my mind and working with ideas. It's not that I'm precious—I like raking leaves and even vacuuming the floor—but I just don't like to work with my hands. They're clumsy. Once when I was eleven I made a picture which won a prize. I did it in crayons in about four colors, and I really worked hard at it for two afternoons. I persisted on it. I remember it was a sailboat. I got a sense of satisfaction out of it, but I don't get as much satisfaction from what I do with my hands as from what I do with my mind. I simply don't get *any* satisfaction out of potholders!

Charles Roberts

Charles Roberts was born thirty-three years ago in Corbin, Ky. At the age of six, he entered the Kentucky School for the Blind. He was graduated from high school in 1944 and, in 1953, he received his B.A. from Miami University in Ohio, where he was elected to Phi Beta Kappa. He also holds a Master's degree. Along with an avid interest in music and an extensive record collection, Mr. Roberts has a broad background in history, classical literature, economics, politics, baseball, and Elizabethan drama. He has written scripts for a serious music program on WKRC-FM in Cincinnati. Mr. Roberts is now employed as a dictating-machine transcriber in the Legal Division of the Veterans Administration Regional Office in Louisville, where he lives with his parents.

I was born blind, and no one has been able to explain the cause for this. The blindness does not show; I am tall and have dark hair and blue eyes which appear normal. I have light perception, but efforts to increase my vision have all proved futile. This means that I am a member of a minority group and, to me, this makes two obligations very important. One is not to indulge in the perverse satisfactions that derive from claims to being particularly spiritual or particularly sensitive to sound. (Absolute pitch, for example, has no correlation with vision or the lack of it.) The second obligation is to accept blindness as a *fact*. It is not sensible or possible or useful to try to ignore it. It is by accepting blindness that we learn we must succeed in life in spite of it—or spend our lives crusading for White Cane Week, increased doles from the government, and more stands for the blind.

I am not by nature a go-getter. The philosophy of laissez-faire has always seemed a very pleasing one to me, and if I had been able to indulge in it, I might be quite complacent, even at thirty-three. But I did not have rich parents, and I did not want to use my life for mere subsistence. This meant that I have had to earn enough money for a stable day-to-day livelihood, leisure to pursue my major interests, and even the *hope* of satisfying my whims. Human itchiness being what it is, I know that, if these goals were all attained, it is possible that I might begin to look beyond them. But it is necessary to have a starting point, and I do not always find that the road is clear.

An acquaintance once informed me that the only newsworthy thing about me was that I was graduated from college with straight A's. I still fail to see what that had to do with the price of Corvairs in Constantinople. I have no particular explanation for having done well in my college work; I liked it, and I learned it. At the same time, I am quite aware that any number of students could achieve this record if they cared enough. And this isn't news.

Yet, I think my college days have been the most rewarding days of my life so far. From them I gained several lasting friendships, a personally satisfying education, and at least the potentials for a well-paying job. If my education has not yet paid off in a good position, it has at least partially supplied the state of mind to live decently with economic failure. There is the great esthetic pleasure to be derived from great music and great literature, and there is the capacity to put human existence in some sort of perspective that does not make money the sole criterion of success. These are advantages which I could not have counted on had I not attended a university.

Perhaps what I most enjoyed about college was being part of an enlightened community. Among faculty and students, I escaped the label of "bookworm" and I had real friends with whom I could be serious. Not that I didn't participate in dormitory shenanigans —I did, in spite of the frowning objections of a couple of earnest vocational counselors. I count these among my best memories.

And so I got my B.A. and my M.A. and I started to work. I did not live happily ever after. Sometimes I remind myself of something a teacher once said: "The truth is seldom black or white; it's some shade of gray." I suppose some people will be surprised that this remark could mean much to a blind man, but it often does serve to remind me that my life is not unrelieved personal tragedy; it is not that black.

There is, for example, the satisfaction of knowing that I do my work well. I was hired as a transcribing machine operator (governmentese for typist), and I have remained in this position for six years. The work is not particularly taxing physically, but it is monotonous. In spite of the fact that there is no mental challenge in any of my days, I have done my job conscientiously, and, in their way, my employers have rewarded me for this. I can expect a yearly rating of "outstanding." I have received a Presidential Committee Citation as an outstanding handicapped worker. The Governor's Award for Kentucky's Outstanding Handicapped Citizen was given to me in 1956. I have been written up in newspapers and other publications.

Although the people I work with are not particularly stimulating, they are quite agreeable and easy to get along with. I am sure that I have not incurred much malice. But what I have met is much worse: ignorance and indifference which keep me on a treadmill. I happen to feel—even to know—that I am capable of doing work which is much more meaningful, much more remunerative, and, above all, much more in line with what I am and what I can do.

I have resorted to every honorable means I know to break this log-jam. I have taken and passed the Junior Government Assistant test which was, at that time, the most difficult test given by the government, and I have constantly repeated to our personnel officials that I want consideration for promotion. I have been recommended for the promotion that I feel I deserve by a number of influential people.

I am aware that, in any good position I fill, there would have to be provision for a stenographer-secretary or similar assistance, but I also have reason to believe that I could do such a job well. I am entitled to at least a *chance* to show what I can do. Many of my co-workers, with less education and a lower intelligence quotient, get such chances and make good at them. Stereotyped, routine work is not the work I can do with the pleasure that supplies real creative energy to a job.

I have received all the answers that occur to the ill-informed or the indifferent. The first approach has always been that while they think highly of my talents and qualifications, the terrible fact remains that I am blind. During these discussions, my record is forgotten. They dangle before me the possibility that my position can be upgraded, but they manage, at the same time, to insinuate darkly that I should be grateful to have work at all. (Ordinary logical processes never intrude upon these discussions.) The second approach pretends to be legal in character. There is the Whitton Rider which forbids by law any drastic grade jumps. I remind them that there is a loophole in this rider, as there is in all the federal regulations I know about—a loophole which provides for exceptions upon the recommendations of the administrator to the Civil Service Commission.

In outlook I suppose I am mildly pessimistic. I do not mean to suggest that I am despairing—I have been labeled "a pleasant cynic" and a "realist," whatever that is. Perhaps it is just that I am not a crusader. My day-to-day life is not unpleasant. I have a stable home life, plenty of excellent music, enough human companionship—and enough sense to know that this is a great deal.

And I have not lost hope that I will get ahead. Recently we had a change of management at our regional office. The new manager is sympathetically and intelligently aware of my existence, and he has assured me that I will not be forgotten. No matter how often we are rebuffed, and no matter how thick our skins grow, we still like to hear things like this. The world still lives on hope, after all.

Incidentally, I am sure that the picture I have presented is only *my* side of the coin. I may have failings which have complicated matters. I hope to find out what they are and, above all, to be able to correct them. The world is not against me, and I am not yet against the world.

Dorothy Petrie Fein was born in Rockland, Me., in 1923, a victim of cerebral palsy. When she was five years old, her family moved to Portland, where she attended school. At Bates College she was elected to Phi Beta Kappa, and was graduated *cum laude*. After she received her M.A. from MacMurray College, she worked as a statistician for five years and then came to New York to work as a recreation leader in a play-school program for cerebral-palsied children. In addition to being a wife and the mother of two children, she has done volunteer work in a hospital and created many of the properties for a local opera company.

Dorothy Petrie Fein

Although I was delivered at the end of a normal pregnancy, I was born with my throat paralyzed. Hemorrhage and convulsions followed, and I was not expected to live. I was over a week old before I was able to make my first sound. After that, my development was normal, and I was an active child, alert, and talking before I learned to walk. Although I never crept, I used to move rapidly about the house with a sliding-hitching combination in which my weight rested alternately upon my buttocks and the back of the head, and I delighted in kicking vigorously when lying in my carriage.

The permanent effects of my birth injury became apparent when I learned to walk, which wasn't until the age of two and a half. Instead of taking slow, deliberate steps, I ran directly across the room at high speed, stopped only by a crash into some intervening object. As I was slowed down, a peculiarity of gait was noticed. When doctors realized that nothing could be done for this, they advised therapeutic exercises, some of which involved walking along a straight line to bring my feet closer together, standing on one foot to improve balance, leg-lifting from the hips while lying flat on my back, and bicycle pumping in the same position.

I spent many childhood hours doing exercises to train my fingers to move independently of each other. Some of these required intense concentration. I experienced much frustration watching four fingers move involuntarily along with the one finger that I wanted to move, and when I tried to separate the fingers, I blocked, preventing any movement at all! As the exercises progressed from simple movements to more appealing ones, such as stringing beads, I felt less tension. When I was relaxed and unhurried, I was rather successful in the use of my fingertips, but whenever I tried to rush or concentrate too hard, I was not able to do as well.

As I grew older, these exercises were supplemented with muscle-training toys, such as building blocks and modeling clay. Quite often I was exhausted and irritated by the blocks, but they taught me the need for repeated effort and calm, unhurried control in any motor activity. Under the tension of forming clay figures, grasping pressure was exaggerated and the soft clay was either crushed in the palm of my hand or broken by a swift, unsteady movement of my arm. Although I enjoyed rolling and kneading the clay, I was never able to make figures from it.

I always had the awkwardness of a much younger child when I played ball, and the slowness with which I brought both hands together in catching made it difficult for me to hold even a fairly large ball. Throwing and rolling a ball consisted of an undirected push, executed with considerable force but poorly aimed. Faulty muscular coordination handicapped me and I had trouble gauging distances. Balls aimed at me would frequently bounce off my body before I could bring my hands up into a catching position. It was only through repeated practice at such games as table tennis and deck tennis that I was able gradually to solve this problem.

When I was five, my family moved, and I had the double problem of adjustment to a new neighborhood and to the first grade of public school. Because of my handicap, I was ridiculed in the playground, and I was restless and ill at ease in the classroom. I developed all sorts of fears—of the dark, the policeman, the bogey-man, guns, being left alone, and sudden death. Finally I was removed from school for a year, and during this time I was prepared for school more gradually. A year later, upon my return, I adjusted more readily. Wise parents encouraged the friendship of a local police officer, the use of a small flashlight at night, and the firing of a Fourth of July pistol to counteract my fears.

Although I was advanced beyond the rest of my class in reading, I had difficulty with my handwriting. This caused me much distress in the early grades because of the emphasis put on motor skills and attractive penmanship.

My personality was probably most fully developed in the years between ten and eighteen. During this time, I developed sufficient command of my body, and confidence in myself as an individual, to have a normal play life and to be accepted by a social group of my own age and a few older friends. I mastered my childhood fears, and I became an omnivorous reader. My interest in the world around me was growing prodigiously, and I felt that perhaps it might be good for me to join the Girl Scouts.

Membership in this organization played an important role in my physical, social, and mental development. I learned to weave, darn, cook, mend, share housekeeping responsibilities, and use a sewing machine. Such things as playing folk songs at reduced tempo on the piano, first with a few fingers of my left hand and later in full score, improved my manual dexterity. It was at this time that I came to appreciate the value of hiking and walking, and these became a desirable and enjoyable form of recreation. At one point, I accompanied my group on a seven-mile hike without any ill effects. I was even developing a better sense of rhythm and bodily grace through the scout activities of folk-dancing, archery, and dramatics.

In troop entertainment and social service projects I learned to distinguish between the things that I could do successfully and those that others could accomplish more efficiently. I was quite at ease in social situations, enjoyed people, took responsibility well, and devised my own techniques for keeping up with others, who gave no outward attention to my physical handicap and frequently recognized me as the group leader. I can thank my scouting experiences for stimulating me socially and culturally, and for creating a sense of belonging and individual worth.

My parents, feeling that any attempt on their part to overprotect me would lead only to increased dependence, insisted from the beginning that I learn to make my own decisions and solve my own adjustment problems, and they gave me a wider scope of personal freedom than many of my friends. I can now look back and say that this psychological independence and freedom was one of the most important factors in my attainment of poise and my sense of personal adequacy.

I was quite outgoing as a child, doing everything with energetic enthusiasm, and since I expended greater effort than normal children, I ate heartily and slept soundly, which was essential for my motor control. When fatigue, excitement, haste, or nervous tension undermined this control and released a stream of involuntary movements, my muscles became rigid and I could accomplish nothing. On the other hand, when I tried to sit quietly, or read, my left shoulder would start to tremble. It frequently occurred during class discussions when I was very interested or personally concerned with the topic, but it always stopped if I was called on to recite. It didn't disappear until my college years, to be replaced by a slight unsteadiness in performance which is less embarrassing and easier to control.

Throughout high school I was generally regarded as a leader among my classmates. My biggest handicaps were the slowness and poor legibility of my writing, and quick exhaustion in taking class notes. Since time is an important factor in dealing with discussion questions on exams, I was frequently given a few minutes of extra time to finish. But even under these conditions, I condensed my answers into terse, telegraphic comments, hurried almost to a point where all movement was blocked, and very often I had to take time out to relax my hand and arm between questions. I was often completely exhausted by the prolonged effort and tension involved in writing an exam.

My unsteady arm and jerky walking made it difficult to carry such things as food trays, and I had further difficulty in opening a full milk bottle or eating an ice cream cone or a piece of cake. But as time passed, and I became less self-conscious about eating with others, my eating problems decreased and recurred only at social functions, where there was always a temptation to decline refreshments rather than risk the chance of crumbling or spilling them. This problem was gradually solved by taking half servings of liquids and going into a quiet corner to eat. However, I still hold my arm close to my body for steadiness in holding liquids.

During high school, I avoided dances, socials, and school athletics in favor of participation in a wide variety of extracurricular activities: glee club, yearbook, science club, French club, and Red Cross. During my junior year I took a fifth, unrequired subject, because biology was not a regular part of the college-preparatory course.

The one disappointment in high school was being barred, because of slow, unclear speech and athetoid movements, from delivering the debate cases which I took great delight in preparing. On one occasion, I watched a teammate lose a rebuttal because she had misplaced the card containing my argument! I was also quite annoyed at being excused from gymnasium, which I thoroughly enjoyed. Both these "sad experiences" have since been compensated for by public speaking before large young adult church groups in New York City (my speech, I am told, becomes amazingly clear under such stimulation) and by four happy years of physical education at college during which I learned to respect my body and to use it with a new feeling of beauty and joy.

In college, extracurricular activity and social functions merged. Department club meetings and discussion groups in faculty homes were followed by tea and cookies. In the warmth of this environment, I relaxed and enjoyed the refreshments, which were thoughtfully placed on a table or chair to put me at ease in the managing of them. The combination of acceptance and loss of self-consciousness produced a new ease in coordination. By the time I reached graduate school I was sufficiently secure in my control to enjoy afternoon teas and similar social functions.

One of the happiest aspects of my college career was the willingness of my parents to open their home to other students. The college years were also rich in opportunities for leadership: discussion groups, Y.W.C.A. story hour, a current events program in the local high school, poetry club, English club, a Sunday school class were a few of my outlets. There was more competition here, more rivalry for achievement, but also more and richer peer relationships and more opportunities to share and to cooperate with those of similar interests and abilities.

Because of my varied interests, I had never had the problems that many handicapped people have in being accepted, but now understanding was added, and the social side of my personality flourished. Relationships wtih the opposite sex were now based on common interests rather than physical graces, and I began to dare to form friendships here as well. I enjoyed esteem and affection from faculty and students alike and was frequently sought out for comfort and counsel, a role which enhanced my security and helped to make up for what I felt I had missed in being an only child. This extroverted orientation has been useful in later life, as I have found that approaching new situations and people with a willingness to use whatever I have to give greatly helps to overcome self-consciousness and to facilitate adjustments. It is a role, however, which one must sometimes be able to lay aside in order to become a recipient of assistance—and this I have found less easy to achieve.

While in college, I still needed help in setting my hair and cutting tough meat, and with cuffs, high necklines, and back buttons. At graduate school I was completely on my own. I learned to use large curlers, and gradually reduced their size; I bought hook-fastening jewelry, cut my meat on an empty plate before adding vegetables until the technique was mastered, and buttoned all but the top of my blouse before slipping it on. I found that my childhood climbing and my love of an outdoor life had produced a rugged, healthy physique that stood up well under the triple discipline of study, work in a dean's office, and some participation in community affairs.

The preparation of a thesis was supervised by Dr. Henry Halverson, who had previously worked with prehension in children and primates. It consisted of a study of my own motor behavior, with special emphasis on the use of my hands. A series of motor tests was devised and administered under varying conditions and the varying dexterity and steadiness of my two hands compared.

Although I resisted the study strenuously because I refused to recognize any differences between myself and others, the experiment, together with changes in my motor patterns suggested by Dr. Halverson, actually resulted in a better understanding of myself and a better acceptance of the reality of the condition and the need to control it more consciously and more intelligently.

The transition from academic to business world was frustrating. Little recognition was given to my college achievements, my assigned duties rarely exceeded a clerical function, and the institution I went to work in was honeycombed with professional rivalries and personal feuds. I remained in this environment for six and a half years, primarily for the sake of those patients whom I was able to help through personal contact. During this period I joined, with others, a Great Books club and an adult education program. I also found time to catch up on my personal reading, to work more at creative writing, and to participate in a community concert campaign. Weekends at home helped to break the monotony of institutional life.

When the opportunity came to move into professional work with cerebral palsied children in the New York City area, I was most eager to take the opportunity for professional advancement. The change proved a happy one, and the work with cerebral palsied children was not only creative but productive of contacts with other agencies and of learning experiences in shopping, home visits, preparation of reports, trips, and inter-agency conferences. A rich social life and the many assets of the metropolitan area again provided free scope for my personality to expand. Thus the consciousness of any limitations that my handicap may impose becomes lost in my activities and interests. This, I feel, has consistently been the best way of adjustment for me.

After the termination of my work with the handicapped, I moved from the residence club of which I was a member and undertook the responsibility for my own cooking, first in the unused apartment of a friend and now in my own home, where I am learning how to care for my home, my husband, and my two young children.

Melvín E. Schoonover

Melvin Eugene Schoonover was born in Francesville, Ind., on August 22, 1926. A victim of congenital osteogenesis imperfecta, he was repeatedly hospitalized as a child with multiple fractures of the extremities. Without any formal rehabilitation training, he managed to complete his high school education and then went on to Wabash College for his B.A. After graduation from Wabash, he studied for the ministry at Union Theological Seminary in New York. He was also a graduate student in divinity at Union Theological and at Butler University School of Religion in Indianapolis. Mr. Schoonover has worked as a magazine editor and has had some experience in hospital administration. At present he is the Minister at Chambers Baptist Memorial Church in New York, and he also serves as Protestant chaplain at the Hospital for Special Surgery. He enjoys traveling, reading, and stamp collecting. In 1957 he was married, and he now has an infant daughter.

The thing I remember most vividly about my education is how hard it was to acquire. In my case, it was complicated by the fact that a bone disease kept me at home in bed for the first seventeen years of my life. I was born too soon—some years before my state had made any provision for tutoring the homebound, especially those who lived in the country as I did.

In the early years there were the problems associated with laying the groundwork for an education. I had a quick, inquisitive mind, and my family wanted to encourage me to whatever extent they were able. Even though the county superintendent of schools could not provide me with a home teacher, he could at least advise my family about what preliminary steps to take. I still can recall being taught to read with flash cards—strips of paper on which the alphabet had been lettered—and, later on, words of increasing difficulty.

Once I learned to read, there was no stopping me. The superintendent of schools continued his personal interest through the years and regularly provided me with textbooks. The local librarian also helped, and twice each week my grandfather would return home with two new books for me. The librarian, fortunately, had some imagination and sent me a wide variety. I swashbuckled with Rafael Sabatini, rode horses with Zane Grey, and explored little-known parts of the world with Richard Halliburton. There were other, more substantial selections, too, but these were the ones I read most avidly.

Along with my reading went a very meaningful experience of play therapy. My family had provided me—quite unwittingly—with the necessary props: male and female dolls, a miniature house, a farm set, various toy cars and trucks. My indulgent grandmother made elaborate costumes for the dolls and furnishings for the house. The fantasies in which I indulged were varied and vivid. I was to be grateful later for the freedom my family had given me for this kind of play, since it meant fewer emotional problems. It all seems rather amusing now as I look back on it, but then it was with the deadliest seriousness that I played alternately the hero and the villain.

There is no sense in pretending that a growing boy who cannot walk has just ordinary problems. I was able to work mine out, to externalize many of them, to get them *out there* where I could see them, by means of the little world of my toys. If I did not like something in myself, some doll, in a costume to represent the characteristic, was disgraced, or even broken.

All through these formative years, the doctors had dangled before me the hope that some day I would be able to walk. In fantasy I imagined myself as the dashing, handsome prince who conquered the enemy and saved the beautiful princess from yon besieged tower. By my middle teens, I began to lay plans for what I would do when the physical emancipation became a reality.

At about this time a friend of the family suggested that I

should receive some kind of recognition for all the home study I had done and obtain the certificates and diplomas necessary for admission to college. My old friend the superintendent of schools confessed to me later that my letter asking for this threw him into a panic. He did not want to discourage me, but still he could not see how it might be done. Finally he indulged in a bit of buck passing—he wrote to his counterpart on the state level and dumped it into his lap. The reply passed the buck neatly back to him: there was no law to prevent his authorizing a high school diploma, but he would have to determine the means for justifying such action. What I finally did was to take comprehensive examinations in every required grade and high school subject. Grade school was a snap; that took only an afternoon of writing! High school took a year and a half of intensive study. A local high school teacher faithfully led me through examinations, arranged for tutoring in difficult subjects like math, and in general cheered me on when I got discouraged about the whole venture. It is hard to say who was more proud when I finally did receive my high school diploma in 1946.

Along about this time the doctors began to admit, under pressure, that I was not going to "recover." Probably the greatest disappointment of my whole life came the day I received this reluctant admission from my orthopedist. The disappointment was made almost unbearable when he insisted that I should under no circumstances attempt to go to college. The risk, he said, would be too great; I might suffer more fractures in addition to the dozens I had already had. The condition of my bones was such that they were broken very easily, by a jar or fall which would have no effect upon another person. I either had to be so careful all the time that I almost was not living or else take my chances and go through the familiar ordeal of bone-setting once again.

Two people felt my disappointment most keenly. One was the high school teacher, the other my minister. Someone else will have to decide whether they were justified, but they proceeded on a deliberate course to persuade me to defy the doctor's instructions. The minister provided increasingly frequent opportunities to leave bed and home to "try my wings." The teacher dangled the lure of college and a career before me. Finally the die was cast: I began to apply for admission to college.

Then another disappointment came. Every school in my home state refused to consider my application because I would have to get around in a wheelchair. All, that is, except one, which said that, although they were extremely skeptical, they would at least talk about the possibility. First the director of admissions came to see me; then I was asked to visit the campus. I do not think I have ever been so scared in my life as the afternoon I was ushered into an office at the college to face the president, the dean of the faculty, the director of admissions, the professor of psychology, the chairman of the science division, and a few other assorted academic types. For over an hour they questioned me about how I proposed to do this and that. Then they discussed among themselves how each department thought I could meet the requirements physically. Somehow I got through the interview without collapsing and, looking back at it now, I am sure I survived because the realization grew on me that these people were really on my side, that they desperately wanted to be able to say "Yes."

Well, the answer was "Yes." The next four years are a kaleidoscope of impressions. There were times when I resented the demands put upon me; after all, couldn't they *see* I was crippled? Surely some concession should be made. There were other times when I was convinced that things were being made too easy for me, that people were trying to pamper me, and I resented this just as much. The doctors were partly right: I did have more fractures, and these interfered from time to time with my school work. Somehow, though, courses were completed, papers written, exams taken. And friends were made, too. Acceptance came rather quickly; soon students no longer feared to give me a nickname: "The Mechanized Monster." (After it became known that I had decided on the ministry as my profession, the nickname became "The Holy Roller"!)

Despite an automobile accident, which wrecked parts of two semesters, the college stuck by me, and graduation day finally came. There was a huge lump in my throat as my name was called, the students stood, and the president and dean came down the steps from the podium to confer a degree and their best wishes. A day of triumph. Now, I thought, the problems were behind me. Now there would be no problem about getting into a seminary; now there would be no reluctance to employ my skills.

Oh no? Another disappointment was still to come. Seminaries did not seem particularly impressed with my record at college; letter after letter raised the very same objections, the very same reservations, that I had once received from colleges. How in the world, they seemed to ask, could anyone in a wheelchair possibly get along at their institutions? Once again, however, there was a cracked door into which I could push my foot rest: one seminary said "maybe," but quickly added that a personal interview would be required. The president of that institution was visibly impressed when I arrived by Greyhound bus a few months later, having traveled nearly halfway across the country. Still the doubts persisted and attempts were made to persuade me to try elsewhere. My foot rest was still in the door, though, and they finally consented to open the door wide and let me in.

I arrived at the seminary to discover that a dean's assistant had been assigned to "take care" of me. After I had located the nearest bathroom and the most accessible exit to the street and got the general lay of the land in my mind, I politely informed him that I no longer needed his services. Again the pressure of a rugged academic routine; again the experience of alternating between being too soft and too hard with myself, and expecting others to be the same. Somehow courses were completed, papers written, exams taken; and then another day of satisfaction when another degree was awarded and another president came down the steps to wish me well.

In many ways, getting an education has been a hard experience, although I must acknowledge that wonderful people have helped to make it easier. Was it worth it? Certainly. Not only because it did give me some kind of preparation for a job, for a career. Education has made me a more interested person—interested in what is going on in the world, what people are doing. At the same time, it has unquestionably made me a more interesting person.

Handicapped people are never easily received in "normal" society; no one really cares to hear about our operations, no matter how dramatic or gory they may have been. The "whole" are threatened by the "defective," even though most people are unwilling to admit they have such negative feelings. The handicapped person does become something other than an object of curiosity, however, when he can match his wits, his knowledge, and his wisdom against those of others. This has been the greatest gift education has given me: it has helped me to achieve acceptance where it might not have come otherwise, and, as a consequence, I have been able to accept myself a little better.

Harold E. Yuker was born on April 15, 1924, in Newark, N.J., a victim of cerebral palsy. Aside from a ten-month stay at a special training project in Vineland, N.J., when he was fourteen, he received no other hospi-

Harold E. Yuker talization. Upon graduation from the University of Newark, he did graduate work in psychology at the New School for Social Research, and in 1954 he received his Ph.D. in social psychology from New York University. Active in a number of professional organizations, he is past president of the Nassau County Psychological Association. Dr. Yuker is now an associate professor of psychology at Hofstra College and is the Director of Psycho-social Research of the Human Resources Foundation, a division of Abilities, Inc.

In a way, I feel that I do not belong in this book. The reason I do not belong is that I usually do not think of myself as a disabled or handicapped person. I usually think of myself as a psychologist, or a teacher, or a person who likes to talk, or a person with a good sense of humor (some of my friends disagree) but not as a disabled person. In my opinion people are people, and whether they are black or white; Catholic, Jewish, Mohammedan, or Protestant; disabled or nondisabled, is immaterial.

But technically I do belong in this book. I belong here because I have cerebral palsy. It is relatively mild at the present time, but when people meet me they notice that I am physically different. My walk is somewhat strange. My talk is a little slower than other people's. I have some problems with my hands; for example, I must use both hands to lift a glass. I am nervous and jump at sudden or loud noises.

These days most people would consider my disability to be

rather mild. I feel that I can do everything I need to do, and almost everything that other people do. I live alone in an apartment where I am completely self-sufficient. (In seven years I have not broken one dish.) I drive my own automobile. I teach at a college and do various kinds of research. In none of these things do I feel handicapped by my physical disability. Therefore, the question "What does it feel like to be a disabled person?" is a difficult one to answer. Most of the time it doesn't feel like anything. Most of the time I don't feel like a disabled person, I just feel like a person.

This is the way I usually feel, and this is how many other disabled persons usually feel. But I do not always feel this way. Sometimes I am very painfully aware that I am disabled and different because other people force me to be aware of it. At such times I do feel like a disabled person; it doesn't feel good. Let me explain what I mean.

When I feel like a disabled person, I feel I'm different; I'm not the same as everyone else. And feeling that I'm different, I also tend to feel that I'm not as good as everyone else. I don't *really* feel this way, but I do wonder about it sometimes. And I know that some other people think that, because I'm disabled, I'm inferior. These thoughts of being different and inferior often cause me to act in ways that are different. Thus I get myself caught up in a vicious circle.

But most of the time I don't feel different. Most of the time I'm not even thinking about myself; I'm too busy doing other things. When I'm working—either lecturing in the classroom or sitting at my desk or typewriter—there is no time to think about myself. If I did, I wouldn't get my work done. When I am with my friends I am too busy having a good time. When I am reading, thinking about myself would interfere with my train of thought. Thus, most of the time, I think neither about myself nor about my disability.

But I did not always feel this way. When I was younger I was very often made to feel that I was different. My friends didn't make me feel different; it was mostly people who didn't know me. It became a major tragedy to me in my late teens when my friends and acquaintances were all dating and I found myself unwanted—

or so I thought. As I grew older, however, my attitude changed and I began to like myself better and accept myself more readily. This change in attitude gradually occurred because I wanted to change it, and I felt that it was important to change it. I firmly believe that a person can change many things about himself if he is willing to work at it.

I really wanted to be able to forget about being disabled. The main reason was that I had discovered that when I do not think about being disabled, the people around me do not think about it either. (Of course, I am lucky that my disability is not as severe as some people's.) When I am with people I know, I am relaxed, and my disability does not seem to make much difference; but when I am very self-conscious or nervous everybody else seems to be conscious of my disability, and things go from bad to worse.

My mother and father helped make it easy for me to change my attitude. They encouraged me to believe in myself and my abilities. I was not spoiled; instead, I was encouraged to do things for myself. My mother taught me to have self-confidence and to evaluate myself realistically. Without these attitudes on the part of my parents, I doubt whether I would ever have achieved self-acceptance.

Various problems confronted me as I grew up, and many decisions had to be made. It was necessary to decide whether or not to go into a hospital for an extended period of time, whether to select a vocation or to get a job. These problems were not unique to me, nor were they problems that only disabled people face. They were problems that everyone has to deal with in one way or another. Disability may have made the problems a little more difficult to solve, but it did not create them.

These problems were not easily solved, but I was very fortunate to have parents who helped me reach decisions instead of making them for me. All decisions were made by me and me alone, even when I was twelve and fourteen years old. My parents discussed my problems with me and voiced their opinions when I asked them to, but they insisted that the final decision was my own responsibility.

The question of therapy keeps cropping up. It was not a problem in grammar school, since I attended a school for crippled children in which physical therapy was part of the curriculum. Upon graduation, however, it became necessary to decide whether or not to attend a high school that had special facilities for disabled children. I decided to attend a regular high school instead, and therapy ceased.

Then, when I was fourteen, the question arose again. I was offered the opportunity to be a patient at a special experimental treatment unit for boys with cerebral palsy. My parents were asked whether they wanted me to go, but they threw the problem into my lap. I decided to try it. After a month or two I regretted my decision. Because I was very unhappy, lonely, and sorry for myself, I ran away. Ten hours later the police brought me back and my mother was called in for a three-way conference with Mr. Thomas McIntire, the director of the treatment unit. I now had to decide whether to stay at the hospital or to go home. I decided to stay, and the next ten months spent at Babbitt Hospital in Vineland, N.J., resulted in a dramatic improvement in my physical condition.

When I left Vineland, I went back to high school. That was the end of physical therapy for me. I am quite certain that my physical condition would be better than it is if I had continued a regular program of exercises. Even today much could be done. It is just that I never seem to get around to it.

At the age of ten I was given a small chemistry set, and soon I was completely immersed in chemical experiments. I managed to experiment my way from a one-dollar set-up to the giant ten-dollar model (a prize for selling several hundred copies of *The Saturday Evening Post*) without causing extensive damage either to life or to property. This interest was furthered in high school by a chemistry course and by a part-time job in the high school chemistry lab. I decided to be a research chemist.

Consequently, when the time came to go to college, I enrolled for a course in chemical engineering. Various tests indicated that this was a wise selection, but two weeks at the Newark College of Engineering taught me differently. I found that my muscular coordination was not nearly good enough to get me by in either mechanical drawing or delicate lab work. Luckily, I was able to make a quick switch and I wound up as a major in business administration at the University of Newark.

Once or twice I wondered about the wisdom of this "quick switch." Perhaps if I had stuck to it and shown perseverance I might have made the grade. But would it have been worth it? It would have proved something, but I didn't feel that that something needed proving. I don't feel that it is necessary to prove I can do anything that I set my mind to. I am satisfied that I can do some things well and that I can get along as well as the next guy. This does not mean that I am not ambitious or that I think ambition is bad. But I do feel that our aspirations should be reasonable and should proceed a step at a time. It is better to be encouraged by reaching near goals than to be discouraged by failing to reach your goals because they are still far off.

Several years ago I talked to a young man with cerebral palsy who wanted to be a surgeon. "Other CP's have made the grade, why can't I?" When he was questioned as to why he wanted to be a surgeon he revealed, perhaps unknowingly, that it was just a challenge—he just wanted to prove that he could do it. This is a very poor basis for choosing a profession. I think the person who is always trying to prove something is a pretty unhappy individual, and the odds are great that he will never succeed in proving it.

But it seems to me that often a profession is not chosen at all— you just seem to fall into it. At least that is the way it happened to me. The switch from a B.A. in business administration to a Ph.D. in psychology was not the result of any quick and simple decisions.

Upon graduation from college I obtained a clerical job with a government agency. After two years I was quite bored and decided to take some courses. Psychology seemed interesting. I did well in the courses and soon found myself working toward an M.A. in psychology, "just for the hell of it."

But then the government agency moved out of town and I was out of a job. Several months later I landed a ten-hours-a-week job at the Bureau of Applied Social Research at Columbia University.

Soon this expanded to twenty hours a week and I was offered a scholarship and a fellowship to continue my studies in psychology at the New School for Social Research. Although the combined income didn't compare with my government salary, I was satisfied. Thus, for the second time, I found myself attending college because I couldn't get a job. Fortunately, this time, my education led to a good job—otherwise I might have been one of the best educated persons ever to die of starvation.

In my opinion one of the major problems that a disabled person—any disabled person—faces is that of getting a job—any job. This problem plagued me from the time I was graduated from high school until the time I was close to my Ph.D. Furthermore, I have no guarantee that it will not be a problem again some time in the future.

When I was graduated from high school I started looking for a job. Since I had no special skills, I would have taken almost anything; but there did not seem to be anything available. One morning, after getting up at 4:30 A.M. to apply for a job, I was lucky enough to be one of twelve men selected to deliver breakfast cereal samples from door to door. I worked from 7:30 to noon delivering samples. At noon I was fired by the area supervisor, even though my crew chief said I had done a good job. Reason for the firing: the company couldn't take chances on a disabled person.

I did not get a job all summer, and toward the end of August my vocational counselor suggested that I go to college. Since my college tuition would be paid by the state rehabilitation division, I decided to go. Although this was not a good basis for making it, the decision turned out to be a wise one.

The job problem recurred during my third year in college when I applied for a summer job with the federal government. The employment interviewer sent me to five department heads who had openings for clerical workers; none of them could use me. The sixth department head hired me—to run a mimeograph machine. Thus, my disability kept me from getting white-collar jobs for which I was qualified, but it did not keep me from getting a low-level manual job for which I had no qualifications and which I was not at all sure I could handle. I soon found out, however, that I could run a mimeograph machine quite adequately.

It is quite apparent that this is a typical situation. The disabled person has trouble getting a job whether he is qualified or not, but it is easier for him to get a low-prestige, unskilled job than a relatively high-level job for which he may be better qualified. In other words, it is usually desirable, and often necessary, for the disabled person to be overqualified for a particular job. Only if he is obviously quite superior to all the other applicants will he be able even to compete for the job. It is not enough to be average or slightly above average.

This holds true in other areas as well. Often the disabled person, in trying to get along, finds that he may not be merely as good as anyone else, but that he must be quite a bit better. Therefore he must find out what his aptitudes are and stress these rather than attempt to be good at everything. And this principle, just like all of the others that apply to disabled persons, applies equally well to the nondisabled individual.

Richard Moore

Richard Moore was born with cerebral palsy in Battle Creek, Mich., in 1926. Here he attended an experimental school endowed by W. K. Kellogg. After high school and four years at Olivet College, Mr. Moore went on to graduate study and earned his Ph.D. in biology. He is now a professor of biology at Hardin-Simmons University.

When I was born in 1926, the phrase "cerebral palsy" had not been conceived and we were all called "spastics." I suppose the conditions in Battle Creek, Michigan, were like those in most other parts of the country. The prevalent ignorance did me less than usual harm, perhaps, because of my good fortune in being able to attend a public school which did not segregate me except for treatments designed to improve my condition.

Not that everything was easy: from the third grade on I had to do everything on the typewriter, and I can remember doing long division without being able to see the whole problem at once. I do not know whether this added or subtracted from a somewhat dubious mathematical ability. In the ninth grade I took penmanship and spent an hour every day, five days a week, practicing the writing of my name. Apparently it was not worth it, since I still do not write except to sign checks; even here I have trouble and must go to the same window of the same bank each time I want a check cashed. I have no checking account and do not even use traveler's checks. My students apparently have no trouble reading number and letter grades which I put on their papers, but I do not attempt corrections in any detail. Ball point pens are a boon to people with cerebral palsy; I used to bend the points of the choicest pens of my best friends—one way to be real popular!

I do not know exactly why, but I took a college preparatory course at school. I do not remember being concerned in those early days about the choice of a profession. At the end of my junior year at high school I went to a hospital school near Detroit for a three-month evaluation peroid. I don't remember very much about this except that I was very homesick and I cried a lot. The evaluation itself was not particularly helpful. I was advised to go to college, but no suggestions were made about what I should study most or why. I did, however, meet a teacher there who had gone to Olivet College and whose father had been a member of the staff for many years. I decided that I wanted to go to Olivet, and I could not have made a wiser choice.

I enrolled in the fall of 1944 and decided on chemistry as a major. I had great respect for the chemistry teacher at Olivet and fully enjoyed my first year's work there. I returned to Battle Creek with the idea of trying to find a job. A local company at first agreed, but when I asked for a typewriter to fill out the application blank, their attitude changed. I was crushed. That bus ride home was the longest I have ever taken. I was later to learn that I would always have a hard time getting a job. It was a common experience to find that employers put the fact that I had cerebral palsy far ahead of any consideration of my ability to do the work.

After that first experience, the workers from a state rehabilitation agency suggested that I change my major. When I refused to do so (I had done well in the subject and I liked it), they took up the matter with the administration of the college. The dean stood by me all the way. For me, it was no longer a question of what my major field should be but a matter of deep personal pride.

Because of the requirements of the laboratories, the physical effort was terrific. Quantitative analysis was particularly difficult because of the precision which was necessary: we had to weigh to the 1000th of a gram. Invariably I would spill the substance as I took it off the balance, and the whole nerve-wracking process would have to be done over. In the end, though, I became expert in quantitative analysis, and I still remember a lot of it. I never failed to appreciate the consideration given to me by the chemistry teacher. He took the time, for example, to read my examinations written in longhand. Typing an examination in organic chemistry would not be possible.

I took so much biology as well as chemistry that I had a double major in college. I also completed two years each in physics and mathematics, so I had a double minor. I realize that my schedule was heavy on the science side and that this might not have been permitted in any other college. I had very little time to do anything else, although I got a little German, which later proved to be helpful.

During my senior year at college, I began to be concerned about finding employment. There were three other students at Olivet who had cerebral palsy, and they were having as little success as I was in finding a permanent position. I wrote to one chemical company I knew of about a position, and results were discouraging. Then I applied to other places. I showed every answer to the dean, who continued to be interested and hopeful for my success. At the end of the school year, however, I had nothing to show for my efforts. I was desperate. One day the dean called me in and offered to let me return to Olivet as a teacher in biology. Olivet College did not give rank to any of its teachers, but I suppose the job he offered me was something like a graduate assistantship. It paid $900 a year, and out of that I had to pay for board and room, but it was a job and I was elated.

The summer after my graduation the administration at Olivet changed, my good friend the dean resigned, and I was appointed to assist a new young biology teacher from New York. However, it was made clear to me that the position was not renewable and that there would be no place for me on the teaching staff the following year. The one year was wonderful, though, and it was enough to settle my choice of a profession. I wanted to teach and nothing else.

Of course, this meant graduate work and I began seeking ways and means of managing the expense of it. The State Vocational Rehabilitation Agency had no funds for graduate work for me. My folks were able to help me and I had saved a little from my salary at Olivet. Of course, I wanted to earn as much as I could in the summer.

I filled out an application blank for a job as a camp counselor. I did not mention on it that I had cerebral palsy or any handicap at all for that matter. I should never have made this omission because in almost every case it leads the handicapped person into embarrassing or humiliating situations. But in this one case, my references must have been satisfactory, because I was accepted.

When I got to camp, however, I met a very startled and shocked camp director. He was in a delicate situation: I had a contract; he was short of counselors; but I obviously was not what he had expected. He decided to let me stay, and he gave me a cabin of eleven-year-olds. However, he insisted that a relief counselor stay in the cabin with us. After two periods he put the relief man somewhere else, and I had won a moral victory. I was made assistant nature director because of my biology background, and after subsequent summers in other camps, I directed the nature program for my first employer for three years. He has, however, inserted a blank on his application forms where any physical handicap must be mentioned.

I did my graduate work at Michigan State in zoology. My adviser was an elderly man about to retire; but he was quite active at that time and still is. He had no sympathy for my wish to teach, and he insisted that research was the only practicable work for me. During my second year, I asked him for a graduate assistantship, and he replied, "My students have to dissect frogs in their work in zoology, but they do not have to accept you as a teacher."

Of course, as one proceeds through life with a handicap, one becomes accustomed to this kind of remark and usually makes pretty fair adjustment to it. However, it always comes as a shock when it is spoken by a person whose intelligence or civility one has taken for granted. When I am back at Michigan State, I always look up this old man. He remembers me, but he has never apologized for his words to me; possibly he has forgotten them by now.

I was interested in the morphological phases of zoology, and the professor in that field was a man to whom I have had every reason to be grateful during the years. I studied zoology and bio-chemistry for a year and a quarter, then changed fields and completed my work in the Veterinary Anatomy Department. I shall always remain indebted to the chairman of this department, both for her personal encouragement and for the opportunities she helped make possible for me. She offered to let me assist her in an embryology course I had previously taken with her. Although she had no graduate assistantship to offer me, she arranged to give me a little graduate credit for my work. She reminded me that I must not drool on the students' microscopes as I assisted them. She had previously cleaned off mine on a couple of occasions; it was hard for me to avoid this when my head was tilted down to look at slides.

The following year she did manage to get a graduate assistant-ship in anatomy for me. I was at camp when her offer came, and I could not send my acceptance back fast enough. I held that job for four years and enjoyed it very much.

For my dissertation, I chose to compare the bladders and the proximal urethras of the domestic animals. Part of the material was already sectioned and was available to me for study, and I enjoyed getting the rest from the postmortem laboratories. I'm only five feet and one inch tall, and I could almost get lost while searching for a urinary bladder among the "innards" of a dead cow or horse. Sheep, goats, hogs, cats, and dogs were easier.

Just before the beginning of my fifth year as a graduate assistant, I was offered an opportunity to go to Hardin-Simmons as an assistant professor of biology. My parents feared that I had bitten off more than I could chew, but a week after the offer, I was on my way by plane to Abilene, Texas.

I learned that I would teach general zoology and all of the morphological areas of biology, along with physiology. Later I was to teach microbiology and general botany. I had little work in microbiology and I had never had a course in botany. I've taught botany three times now, and the fact that I am repeatedly asked to teach it is a source of genuine satisfaction to me. At the end of my first year at Simmons I returned to Michigan State to complete the doctorate, and it was awarded at the end of the summer. The university granted an increase in salary for a year of successful teaching and the attainment of the doctorate. At the end of the second year I became an associate professor in biology, the position that I now hold.

My work with the student nurses has been especially gratifying to me. At the end of my first year I was assigned as their counselor, advising them while they are here as preclinical students and, when they finish their clinical training and come back to work on their bachelor's degrees, I again counsel with them and work out their degree plans. I also teach them anatomy and physiology and micro-biology. I have come to know all of them very well and I appreciate the honors that they have bestowed upon me. At the end of my first year, they asked me to be their speaker at their capping service, and last year they dedicated their yearbook to me. I have been in the homes of many of them and have come to know their parents, in all parts of the state, quite well.

I take pleasure in being a part of the academic life of this University. I enjoy my committee work very much, and I am sometimes asked to serve as sponsor on various extension trips and to serve the University in other ways.

In Lansing, Michigan, I was a member of the local United Cerebral Palsy chapter and served it in various capacities. I have spoken on cerebral palsy to various campus groups; classes in special education and speech correction require knowledge of this kind. I, myself, am principally concerned with the causes of cerebral palsy, the orthopedic management of it, and the correction of certain public misconceptions concerning it. I am convinced that society underestimates the usefulness of the person born with a physical handicap and, in many cases, deprives itself of the benefit that this brain power can bestow upon it. The estimate of a person's ability to contribute to society should obviously not be based either upon his appearance or upon a few superficial interviews. As a biologist, I know that human beings are more complicated than this, and as an individual interested in human progress, I deplore the waste of knowledge and skill which results from inadequate or mistaken judgment.

I thought for many years that I could not drive a car. When bus service became poor in Abilene, I called a man who teaches driving privately. He took me out and let me try, told me that I could drive, and proceeded to teach me. This was one of the best $50 I ever spent. After learning how to drive and passing the driving test, I bought a car. This has opened up new worlds to me. I have trouble carrying as much insurance as I wish, but I have a sympathetic agency which has been able so far to carry it for me. This is another example of people's reluctance to accept the judgment of the individual involved and the statistics on handicapped drivers. Repeatedly prejudice, instead of sound judgment, operates against a handicapped person who is attempting to get something done. I would not drive if I thought that I would endanger my life or anyone else's. I have driven many thousands of miles in a short three years, and I have a spotless driving record. My only trouble seems to be in keeping out of the way of "normal" drivers.

Summers constitute quite a problem to me, and the pleasure of driving has helped with this. But as I write this in August, I am eager to get back to my classes again. I think I was right about being a teacher; this *is* my pleasure as well as my work. I think I can honestly say that the people along the way who could not see it were wrong.

Ralph Englert

Ralph Englert was born in Nashville, Tenn., in 1938. At the age of seven, he was stricken with spinal meningitis, which left him totally deaf. He learned lip reading at the Nashville League for the Hard of Hearing and later studied at the Bill Wilkerson Speech and Hearing Foundation. Upon graduation from high school, he entered Middle Tennessee State College, majoring in English and minoring in sociology and physical education. Mr. Englert is interested in sports and was sports editor of *Midlander*, his college yearbook.

I became a citizen of "the silent world" at an early age. I was too young to realize all the implications and consequences of the ordeal through which I had passed. It was good to be back from the hospital, good to be with my family again, and they certainly made me feel that my deafness made no difference in their affection for me or in their hopes for my future. Friends of the family and our neighbors were casual and kind and encouraging. In my room, alone, I was more puzzled than anything else, realizing that without sound the world was different, but not quite knowing *how* different it would be.

I had left the second grade at the time of my illness, and when the day arrived to return to class, I had my first encounter with the peculiar fear and anxiety that, since then, has become all too familiar. I was sick at my stomach at the same time that I was hoping with all my heart that my classmates would accept me as they had before my deafness. My mother went to school with me that first day. We stood together in the door of the room I had left as a happy-go-lucky, anybody, boy. I hardly had the courage to look at the familiar faces, but gradually I *did* look, up and down each aisle, from one child to the next. They all looked back at me, and I wondered what they were thinking. Then it happened: as my glance cautiously approached my vacant seat and then stopped at the face of the little boy who was sitting beside it, he grinned and waved a greeting to me and then beckoned me to come and take my place among them all again. I suppose that, without exactly knowing it, I had been waiting for this gesture for many weeks. The little boy is a man now, and I wonder if he knows the importance of what he did for me. I guess I remember the incident so gratefully because it had become so necessary for me to know that I could become a member of a group again.

There were many other times that were not so happy. It is, of course, impossible for a totally deaf person to know whether or not people in a group are talking about him. This uncertainty is a problem to all deaf people, but I think I was particularly sensitive. I tried to work on this, to achieve some personal independence about it, not to care so desperately. I cannot honestly say, in spite of all the hours of self-examination and effort, that I am completely free of this kind of social insecurity.

My family has never failed me in times of discouragement or despair. The fact that I have always been able to count on them has made it easier to try to find my own way. Even my father, who is a sick man, has given me advice I value, and there is no way to measure the different ways in which my mother has helped me. Not the least of these was the encouragement I was given to try out new experiences for myself, to develop personally and socially and intellectually. They loved me and were interested in me, but they did not overprotect me or burden me with their worry. I used to play every afternoon with the other boys at a playground some distance from home, and on weekends I often went on day-long bicycle trips with my friends. Overnight camping trips stand out among the memories of my growing-up years as more fun than anything else.

People outside my family also helped me from time to time, and Miss Emily Harris, my lip reading instructor, had a great influence on me during the growing years. Our relationship began shortly after I returned from the hospital and continued for about a decade. Although her primary concern was to help me learn the correct pronunciation of words through sentence reading and vowel sounds, her personal understanding helped me in more ways than I can number. Whatever I may accomplish will be, in some way, due to my early association with her. Every handicapped person learns a certain number of things by trial and error, and if the people nearest you let you discover for yourself what you can do, it is a real boon.

In relationships with other people, I find that one of the most disturbing is any group activity, bull-sessions at college, for example. A person who is not deaf almost surely will not be able to realize the intense loneliness of being in a group where the warmth of good fellowship, the enjoyment of wit, and the interest of good talk surround you and can be *felt* but not shared. The loneliest moments I have ever known were in the company of my best friends. Lip reading hardly helps at all on occasions like this. At least among young men, the chief pleasure in bull-sessions is the rapid back-and-forth of quip and joke and word-play.

I read a book once in which a blind man stated that he would rather be blind than deaf. I think he must have been feeling the deaf man's isolation in a group of friends, the isolation which not only prevents his hearing their ideas but, as a result of this apartness, makes it impossible for him to express his own. One need not be deaf and dumb to *feel* deaf and dumb. The blind man can appreciate the wit and intelligence of the friend he cannot see, and it is easier for him to show a friend his own ability to return these invaluable human gifts.

I don't know when it began, but I have discovered that when I accept the existence of a problem, take the time to think it through and find a solution to it, I start to hum a tune to myself, a tune without any words, just a lively melody that gives me a lift and helps me to go on. Since these "songs" make sense to no one but me, I usually hum only when alone or at home with my family. And to this day, I am not sure that even my own relatives understand the meaning of such weird tones. When I once told my sister about this, I explained to her that I have had so many moments of difficulty in the past that I now have a full "album," complete with a tune for each occasion.

I can hardly believe that I have almost completed college. When I entered, the dean warned my family that the school was in no way equipped to educate a deaf boy. My first year was not happy, partly because I could not find anyone to room with and therefore could never be part of dormitory life.

Even the most skillful lip reader cannot get more than a small part of what a professor says from the lecture platform. I had to depend all the way through on the willingness of my friends to lend me their notes, and I had to read my textbooks and collateral work much more intensively than anyone else so that I could make up for what spoken material I had missed. I failed only one course, but I took it again and passed.

During my third and fourth years at college I began to get increasing satisfaction out of writing up sports events for the college paper, and this year, as sports editor of the college yearbook, I have had my greatest pleasure in knowing athletes well. I have liked them very much off the athletic field, and reporting their games has given me so much satisfaction that, after graduation, I am going to try my luck with the newspapers to see if I can get a job sports-writing. I am prepared for some rejections; all handicapped people have to be. They have to try more times than other people. But I have proved I can do this and I know I enjoy doing it. I know it is important for everybody that his work be congenial for him, but I think it is even more important that a handicapped person like his work, because quite often a job plays a bigger part in his life than it does for people with a wider choice of outside interests.

It takes a great deal of sophistication to understand a person with a socially awkward disability which is raw to the eye, dissonant to the ear, and strange beyond social comprehension. I think that it is not the responsibility of society to understand the cerebral palsied, but rather it is our duty to tolerate society and, in the name of chivalry, forgive and be amused by its folly. I find it a dubious honor, but challenging and entertaining. Putting obviously disturbed or curious people at ease before they have a chance to complicate a situation places the handicapped in a role superior to that of the agitators and adds to the human comedy. But this is something it takes a very long time to learn.

BONNIE JANE GARRETT

CHAPTER 4

Friends and Family

The handicapped person must live in the world of nonhandicapped people, and, regardless of how successful his adjustment, his life hinges largely on the response he inspires in others. In the eyes of society, his handicap is as much a part of him as the color of a Negro's skin is a part of him; his handicap becomes both his badge of honor and his brand of shame, and frequently it is both at the same time.

The eight contributors to this chapter deal with their relationships to other people—friends, husbands, wives, uncles, aunts, cousins, acquaintances, and strangers. In the long run, of course, all these relationships depended upon their ability to face themselves, an ability which involved, before anything else, standing in front of the mirror to see exactly what they were. If there is a message in this chapter, it is that the victim of a handicap must attempt to understand himself before he can demand understanding from his friends and acquaintances. He must, in short, emotionally come of age.

Social problems are not, of course, peculiar to the handicapped individual. But it is the fate of the handicapped individual to serve, as Bonnie Jane Garrett was told, as a "catalyst" for other people's "impurities." How many handicapped people do not remember the numerous times they were imposed upon, asked to pity, love, sympathize, smile, weep, hate, scorn, soothe, and help people who were complete strangers to them—and all of it simply because the handicapped person is somehow expected to *understand* other people's problems? If these narratives teach us nothing else, they teach us that the handicapped individual is, at least in part, a creation of his society.

One senses, too, that diseases and handicaps have their own status classifications in the eyes of society. Polio is usually more socially acceptable than, say, cerebral palsy or blindness; somehow it seems to cause the nonhandicapped individual less pain, less confusion, than other handicaps. In this connection, it is interesting to compare the stories told by Sandra Noddin, Joan Hardee, and Bonnie Jane Garrett, a blind girl, a polio victim, and a victim of cerebral palsy.

Sandra Noddin was born on January 5, 1940, in Ayer, Mass. She attended grammar school in Watertown, Mass., and high school in Ayer. Trained at the Rehabilitation Center in Buffalo, N.Y., Miss Noddin is currently

Sandra Noddin

employed as a film-production worker by the Polaroid Corporation. An active member of the Young Women's Christian Association, Miss Noddin attends dances and enjoys ice skating and most other outdoor sports. Among her hobbies are knitting and sewing.

There's so much I want to say I could write a book. It's my whole life. It's why I'm here. But I think sometimes you forget the bad and remember the good. You want to tell people how good you are. I don't want people to know I'm scared to death of a subway, but I do want to tell the way it feels and really is. That's what I want to do.

When I was born, it was established that I was visually handicapped. There was a question of a tumor in the left eye, so it had to be removed. Later it was found out that there was no tumor but that the eye wouldn't ever have been much good to me anyway. The other one was afflicted, but I had travel vision out of it. I never learned to read with it. I could write print if I were slow and careful, but not many people could read it. I went to Perkins School for the Blind, in Watertown, up until the ninth grade. But school was such a big part of my life that I found I wasn't paying any attention to other people, only my blind friends. We were all becoming so much alike that I felt I needed to have more contact with people outside Perkins. I felt I needed the influence of all kinds of people. So I changed to a small public school where the teachers were very nice, and I got along well.

Then, after my first year in high school, it happened. I shall never forget the day I lost my sight or it was apparent, at least, that something was wrong. I noticed that I was having great difficulty seeing in darkened places—in the house and in school and in other buildings. But outside I didn't have much trouble at all. Well, this was the last day of school. We had received our report cards, and the buses hadn't come to pick us up. Another girl and I decided to walk home. On the way we had to go around a rotary. I was used to going to the left, and if I stayed on the sidewalk I could continue bearing left and be on the road home. But this day they had torn up the road at that point, so we had to go around the other way. I had just one more road to go beyond the road that my girl friend lived on, and I would have made it if I could have seen the way. I got lost and had to turn back. I asked the way from some workmen and then continued on home. Later in the day we decided to visit my cousin in the hospital. When we went inside, I kept watching my sister's white blouse in front of me. When the blouse disappeared, I realized it was all I had been able to see. I stood there in the hall like a dummy. That night at supper, I was looking for the mustard. After making several useless attempts to find it, I asked my mother. She showed me where it was and then asked me what was wrong with my eye. Immediately I denied everything. "Nothing," I said. Then I asked her, "Which one?" "You know what I'm talking about. Now tell me." So then it all came out.

The next day we rushed down to the Eye and Ear Clinic in Boston where no one knew the slightest thing about my case. I had doctors crowded all around, waiting for a turn to look. Then a man from Retina Service came and told me to come in to Retina Service the next Monday—there was a doctor in that department who had been studying my case and might have some ideas. I went, and they decided that it was a hemorrhage. He told me that it might be absorbed into the tissues and disappear in a week or so —maybe a month, maybe a year. I decided that of course it was going away right away. So we made an appointment to go back in two weeks. That time we were told to come back in a month. Then next it was two months. Still no change. *Then* it really sank in. They told me a year and then asked me whether or not I realized that I might never see again.

Finding out that I would have to wait a year was what clinched everything. When I heard the doctor say that, I just froze. "A whole year," I said. I was numb until I got home. Then I went up to my room to cry. I had never been a child to cry much, but I cried that night, almost all night long. I felt *so, so* alone. I was the only person in the whole world who could feel this bad. No one could ever understand, ever know what it was like. I was Sandy Noddin, fifteen years old, with almost all of my life ahead of me— and I was to face it without ever seeing again. I was sick. I couldn't eat. I didn't want to face anyone. I came down for supper, but I couldn't talk to anybody, so I went back upstairs again. All through that time when I lost my sight, up to the time when I knew I would probably be this way for the rest of my life, I had lived on hope. "Maybe all of a sudden," I thought, "it will come to me. I might see for Christmas." I thought, "I *have* to see for Christmas. What would Christmas be like if I couldn't see the pretty lights?"

That summer my cousin had come home from the hospital, and my aunt had me come over to sit with her, which meant a little money for me and something to think about. When the time came to go back to school, I refused. I wouldn't go. I'd quit school before I'd go back and face all my friends like this. What would everybody think? What would they say? And, worst of all, what would I do and say, and how would I get around? For two weeks I continued to sit with Gerry, my cousin—and nothing. Then my mother got a call from one of my teachers. "The girls want to know where Sandra is," she said. My mother immediately told her the story of what had happened. That very afternoon two of my best friends came to my house and begged me to come back. They said my being blind made no difference to them and that I was one of them. But I still didn't want to go back. Then the guidance counselor called, and after talking to him I was finally convinced that I should return.

I remember one incident during that summer when my folks wanted to take the whole family to the beach for the weekend. I didn't want to go. I thought I'd spoil it. I'd be a burden to them.

They'd have to lead me around all day and that would spoil all their fun. Why wouldn't they just let me stay home? But they wouldn't. I was *so* angry. I don't know of anybody ever as mad as I was that day. I refused to go. I yelled, screamed, and threw things in all directions. When they made me come out to the car, I tried to run away, but I bumped into the car and hurt my knee. The funny part about it is that I bet I had the most fun of anyone. That whole year, though, I didn't go many places, didn't do much of anything. I had a boy friend who came down to see me and who took me out quite a bit. If it hadn't been for him, I'd probably have gone crazy.

When I started my senior year in high school I had a problem again. The previous year the girls had been leading me around in school. Well, of course our schedules were different, and they hadn't figured out a system. I felt I was a burden to everybody. I tried to quit school again. I wanted to take time off from school and go to Morristown to get a Seeing Eye dog. I applied, but they wouldn't let me leave school. In the meantime, I had notified the state that I was going to public school, and they were planning for me to have a chance at education for employment. They thought I couldn't go right to work immediately after high school. Then they registered me for a cane travel course.

Now, I had seen the old method of using the cane—tapping along—and I rebelled against it. "If you think I'm going to carry a white cane, you're crazy," I told them. I felt that a cane signified blindness, and I didn't want anything to do with blindness. I thought that hiding it made me like anyone else. Even when Mr. Turner, my teacher, came, I told him I wouldn't have a cane. He had a hard time convincing me that it was better to carry a cane and walk around the tree than to make a fool out of myself by bumping into the tree. He helped me see that I'd be less conspicuous and save myself a lot of embarrassment if I didn't try to hide it. Now I've found out that you can't hide it because you show it in your actions.

After I began my cane travel course, things started looking up for me. My teacher had an awful time making me practice, but I really started to have a better outlook on life and to have more fun. I was graduated from high school, and then I came to Cambridge to work. Now I'm never without my cane—I am entirely dependent on it.

Of course, there are still problems in traveling. One of the most humiliating things that has happened to me since I came to Cambridge was falling downstairs in the subway and breaking my wrist. I had just been working about three months, and I felt so stupid. I'm still afraid of subways. I'm afraid of falling downstairs, but I think what makes me most afraid is the subway track. There's no railing on the platform. My cane works according to the law of averages, and it might happen if ever I miss.

I won't ask help in crossing streets, but many people come to me because of my cane. If I want help, I say, "May I take your arm," but if I don't, I say, "Please, I'd rather do it alone." I won't ask anyone who doesn't offer. Recently I had to get a new cane, a longer one, because I walk too fast. I had a problem: I seemed to be veering to the right. I may have to call my teacher for some instruction with the new cane, but I think I can get along myself.

When I came to work in Cambridge for the first time, it was hard. I was working nights. I would wake up in the morning with a sick feeling, thinking about the day ahead. I would have all morning with nothing to do. Then I would have to go to that big restaurant with food that wasn't my mother's cooking. Then all those people, trying to help and getting me confused more and more every minute, and the subway I was so scared of. But I liked work because the people were friendly and it was a challenge to me. I wanted to make a life for myself in the city.

I've found, though, that having a job causes all kinds of problems. It's so hard because you have to fight and fight and fight every minute of the day to prove you *can* do something. I was assigned to work with a group of partially sighted girls—Department X, darkroom worker. It was the big boss who gave us the chance there—the others didn't even think we could work in a darkroom. Can you imagine that! I can do my work well, better than sighted people (I don't mean to be bragging, but this is a fact), and I want to be treated as an individual.

If we handicapped girls have little disagreements among ourselves in the darkroom, the others get upset. We can't even have an argument, a *normal* argument, but it's all right for the others to do it. I want to be employed the same as others and work normally.

I feel such a barrier between me and the normal public. Anything we do, it's because we're different. People who are normal, students reading a book maybe, will walk across a street and almost get run over. I've seen them in Harvard Square. I prove to people over and over that I can do things, and they still don't believe me. Society wants to push blind people together. Why? They have nothing in common. I am a person. I want my individuality.

I've heard people talking about me on buses and subways. They think you're deaf and dumb, too. Once I was out with my teacher, standing on a corner waiting to cross a street. A lady came by and asked him, "Why doesn't she cross the street?" He replied that there was a train going by. "Why, can she *hear?*" the lady asked. It makes me mad that people are so ignorant. One of my strong ambitions is to prove that I'm an individual.

Maybe I should tell something more about myself. I am about five six and a half and have very dark brown hair and dark brown eyes. I have a rather dark complexion, I think. I am on the slender side. As for clothes, I like just about everything. Let's put it this way—I love clothes. I just adore perfume and things like that. When I go home on weekends, my sisters always say, "When are you going to get sick of that so I can wear it?" I wouldn't dare let them look in my clothes closet. I like music and I have bought myself a high fidelity set and quite a few records, both popular and classical. I love hand work. Before I went to work I knitted and sewed things to sell. When I was in school I had all my free periods in the sewing room where I couldn't study, so I sewed. I made all my clothes then. Now I'm lazy, so I buy them, but I've made many sweaters for myself and the kids.

I like most of the things that teen-age girls like—going to movies, ice skating, roller skating, dancing, swimming, sunbathing, and just plain walking in the country. I can enjoy a movie, but I think they're very shallow nowadays: no plot, no story—all romance. Right now I'm taking a course in speech and a course in dancing. I belong to a Y.W.C.A. group (not a blind group) that goes to the air force base to entertain the fellows. I love dancing, but sometimes it's hard going. Some of the fellows hesitate to dance with me because they don't know how to talk with me. I love the city for its busyness and constant activity, and I like the country for its quiet and solemnity, for its freshness and beauty.

And I know what beauty is. One thing I'm very thankful for is that I have seen. I see in my mind. I remember. It's never dark to me in the darkroom. My seeing is like when a normal person goes to bed and sees things in his mind. That's the way I see. In my dreams I can see.

Another of the things I enjoy very much is people. I enjoy my trips to and from work, and any other place I go where I meet people. I always meet them because people are usually trying to help. It is wonderful to see how many different kinds of people you meet. Every once in a while the old ones pop up, and it's like seeing an old friend. I've had some trouble with drunks trying to take advantage of me, and once a fellow at the air force base yelled out to me, "What's the cane for?" But then, I can't stand the ones who are oversweet. They say, "Doesn't she do well!" And I say, "You'd do as well if you cared as much."

Some people worry about how to act with blind people. When I was at the rehabilitation center I met only one sighted fellow, and he took me to a blind party. I was disgusted because I want to meet all kinds of people. But another sighted fellow who asked me out said he hadn't paid any attention to my blindness. He said, "I'm interested in you as an individual, not as a blind person." Sometimes it puzzles me how others can be so interested in our problems. You can always tell when they're really interested because, if they are, they have questions and opinions of their own. I really think people on the whole are wonderful. I love them anyway.

I don't just want a thrill from dancing with a fellow—I want good conversation. This is something very close to me. I'm lonesome—believe me I'm lonesome a lot of the time. But they don't know it on the outside. I go in trends. I have a good spell and then life is a ball. I meet nice fellows, and I go dancing. And then bang. Everything is awful. I can't stop going to the Y because, if I stop, then I lose my courage. But sometimes you think you can't get through it—the slump. I always blame it on my handicap or on my personality. I have times when I'm so low I lie awake at night and cry and wonder what's wrong with me. I wonder why they don't like me. I think, "Other girls make it in the city. What's wrong with me? I'm blind and they don't like me," I say to myself. "I try so darned hard. I'm fighting and fighting. What am I doing here? Why don't I go home?"

I don't really have any close friends. I don't like cliquish people, and I don't like to talk about other people and tell dirty jokes. In the Y there are all kinds of girls. I like them all. I have no enemies but no close friends. One girl who is partially sighted and I try to help each other by talking things out. Some people won't accept constructive advice or criticism. I ask for it, and she's the one who will give it to me.

I lie in bed some nights and I think: "I don't have any place to go tonight. Why not?" And I get curious about people. The man next door goes out. He's happy—he's satisfied with life. I'm not. I want to get out—go to college. When I am unhappy, I make others unhappy. I crave knowledge, and so I ask questions. I want to learn so that I can help the ones who understand less than I do. I want to study psychology. I'd like to go to a coeducational college because I like to be with men as well as women. I wonder whether I can go. Algebra and math were always hard for me because I had to learn the signs in Braille and there was no one to teach me, but I can type and take notes in Braille. And I crave so much to know the things I can't find out alone.

Bonnie Jane Garrett

Bonnie Jane Garrett was born in Kansas City, Mo., on October 8, 1924, a victim of athetoid cerebral palsy. She was not hospitalized until 1958, when she underwent neurosurgery on three cervical disks. Since that time, she has been forced to return to the hospital three times. Miss Garrett's schooling was both varied and extensive. At the University of Kansas City she studied, among other things, directing and playwriting. She spent a year studying sculpture at the Kansas City Art Institute, a year at the Midwest College of Business and Stenotype, and six years studying the piano. Among her hobbies are playing the piano, sewing, cooking foreign dishes, directing plays, and collecting records. Currently employed as the public relations director of the United Cerebral Palsy Fund of Missouri, Miss Garrett also does some free-lance newspaper work and is the publicity director for a local opera company. She has written a book on fashion and grooming for handicapped women. Miss Garrett is single and lives in Kansas City.

As a mildly cerebral palsied cultivated person, I find it difficult to describe cerebral palsy from within. It takes the insight of self-discipline to break down the hard core of proud defense, because talking about this handicap is something like revealing ragged underwear beneath a socially accepted costume.

Having been born an athetoid type of cerebral palsy as the result of a birth injury to the control center of the brain, I was not aware of my startling, complex classification until the term became popular and society insisted that I admit my labeled deviations. It was something like joining Alcoholics Anonymous. You cannot be honest with yourself until you find out what you are and, perhaps, consider what society thinks you are or should be.

Most intelligent people struggle with this riddle and either answer it themselves or go to a psychiatrist.

I did not understand that the difficulties I experienced were in any way connected with an injury at birth. It is certainly true that I did have difficulties, but I was given no means for understanding what they were or how to deal with them. Since my impairment was not great enough to restrain my youthful stamina, the stress of circumstances eventually made it necessary for me to learn about the affliction that had no name when I was born.

Through compensating for my awkwardness with ridiculous feats of endurance, I almost ruined the disks in my cervical and lumbar spine. It took a neurosurgeon, an orthopedist, and an internist three years of surgery, traction, and bracing to put me back in circulation. I did have a lively time during my teens and twenties falling off horses, raising great Danes, and laying bricks, but it would have been cheaper had I been a docile hypochondriac. Joining the United Cerebral Palsy Association was postoperative therapy to counteract over thirty years of ignoring my limitations. I accept them now with aging grace. I believe that the only way to solve a human problem so that it stays solved is to work from what you really are and really can do.

More handicaps have been imposed on me than I could have had unless I were to be run over annually by a truck. One gets used to his own eccentricities, but outsiders seldom choose to realize this because of their own insecurities. The every move of a handicapped person draws more attention than animals at the zoo. My severest, most impressive rejections came when it was time to take an independent, adult role in society.

With one extremely painful exception, as long as I was in the protective custody of family life or college schedules and lived without exercising my rights as an adult citizen, the forces of society were kindly and unruffling. It was after college, business school, and innumerable stretches as a volunteer worker on community projects that I was often bogged down by the medieval prejudices and superstitions of the business world. Looking for a job was like standing before a firing squad. Employers were shocked that I had the gall to apply for a job. Training and experience were ignored, and ambition was considered an inexcusable form of insanity. Volunteer agencies depended heavily on my training as a journalist but never assisted me, when opportunities appeared, by referring my work to an employer. I was generous to a fault, an apology for being handicapped, and I finally had to learn to put a value on my time and work for the sake of dignity.

It is at this juncture that some handicapped people, unprepared for the impact of greed, prejudice, and criticism, withdraw from the outside world of challenge into a sloppy, ambitionless vacuum. The afflicted have to try ten times harder to prove their value to society than the average individual does. I learned to create my own work, sidestepping unnecessary battles with immovable social problems. To me, as a free-lance writer, physical traits are not important, only the ingenuity of the mind. Had I not continued to battle bureaucratic intolerance and found my own special niche, I should have lost dignity and been reduced to basket-weaving. As a cerebral palsied woman, I can never cease rehabilitating my mind and my appearance. Searching for new grooming tricks, corrective exercises, and intellectual challenges is an exciting, stimulating preservative of youth and enjoyment of life.

Cerebral palsy is, for me, a dizziness and pressure at the back of the head which make coordination and balance a never-ending struggle. Under tension, fatigue, or anxiety, I feel that my head may fly off my shoulders. I walk with uncertain steps and often have the sensation of skating over marbles. When tired, I stagger from lack of equilibrium, and I have been arrested twice on charges of drunkenness and once on suspicion of being doped. In the morning when I arise sluggishly, I feel that I have to learn all over again how to propel myself to the breakfast table. Having a weak back, I'd like to climb stairs on all fours instead of two feet, but I never do. Champagne glasses defeat me, but I play Chopin on the piano and have no anxiety about tall drinks or coffee cups. However, I have a natural talent for "tossing salads"—usually on the floor. These inconveniences are mitigated, however, by a constant pursuit of pleasure.

The orthopedic and neurologic oddities never restrained my spontaneous and sometimes explosive participation in each cycle of life. My deep disappointments never outnumbered those of my friends. The men in my life were interesting but slightly weird. In my eagerness for independence, I became engaged only to young men who were incapable of compassion but who depended on mine. Because of their concentrated attention and overpowering devotion to themselves, they became successful in their fields but remained conspicuously unmarried, eminently unloved, and restlessly discontent. Generosity of spirit is the trait of a mature, well-balanced man. I am extremely grateful to them for giving me invaluable and advance training in self-sufficiency, self-defense, and womanly pride. When I outgrew the neurotic necessity to be exploited by egocentric monsters, which was really a way of diverting attention away from my own problems by pretending to be needed instead of needing, a more honest femininity made a happier woman. Not all types of affection are healthy or desirable, no matter how consistent. Unfortunately, only time and experience can teach the handicapped woman to discriminate between sincere devotion and idle experimentation. The degree of healthy self-protection that handicapped people achieve in the area of the emotions indicates the value they place upon themselves. It was once said that we arm people with the weapons with which they hurt us.

It takes a great deal of sophistication to understand a person with a socially awkward disability which is raw to the eye, dissonant to the ear, and strange beyond social comprehension. I think that it is not the responsibility of society to understand the cerebral palsied, but rather it is our duty to tolerate society and, in the name of chivalry, forgive and be amused by its folly. I find it a dubious honor, but challenging and entertaining. Putting obviously disturbed or curious people at ease before they have a chance to complicate a situation places the handicapped in a role superior to that of the agitators and adds to the human comedy. But this is something it takes one a very long time to learn.

It is, however, one thing to think of an abstract public in this light, and another thing entirely to find one's self discriminated against by individual persons who are in positions which require that they have a more informed and understanding attitude. During my teens the cruelty of such ignorance was not unknown to me. I went to school with the rest of the children in my town and always made adequate grades, but one day, when I was thirteen years old, the principal called me into her office and denounced me as a handicapped person who had no business being in a classroom with normal children. That a cerebral palsied child was enrolled in *her* school offended her sense of conformity. She said that I belonged in an institution for mentally retarded cripples. In the mid-nineteen-thirties a verdict of this kind was like a sentence to Devil's Island.

I suppose that this experience was especially painful in part because it came during the sensitive years of early adolescence, but also because, up until that time, I had not *known* that I was handicapped in any sense that could possibly segregate me from other people. No doctor had ever diagnosed my case as cerebral palsy. I had thought I just had certain physical troubles not unlike those of many other people. I was deeply hurt and resentful. Fortunately my indignant parents were able to put me in a girls' school where my pride was mended. But since the principal who rejected me represented a person whose humanity was completely obliterated by her sense of conformity, I ceased to make any efforts to conform. What was there really for me to conform *to*?

And so it was that, in compensatory protest, I became a nonconforming renegade and cavorted leisurely through college. I took it on my own terms, enjoyed most of it, and left after six years without a diploma. I took only courses I liked and nothing else. Classes were small during the war. All my interests and ambitions were encouraged by my professors. They indulged my creative impulses, and I was grateful to find that cultivated, educated people with stable minds did not seem to be uneasy about the eccentricities of speech and gait that I could not control. Among other things, they directed me into a career of writing, which has given me work and personal satisfaction.

Conscripted at birth into the demanding role of a minor public menace and a family disturbance, I learned to have fun with the inquisitive, the curious, and the uninformed. Nobody can enjoy life without being able to see the ludicrous side of society and of himself. The public crises caused by my rolling gait and hesitant speech have enlivened many hours for me. Rude, curious people are probably bored and search for distraction from their drab lives or hope to be shown that someone else will prove to be more of a wreck than they are, for "misery loves company." Reformers and most do-gooders have incredibly dull backgrounds. After three years of college theater training, I've tried to come through with some appropriate dramatic entertainment, and I hope it has amused and cured these people from pestering unprepared cripples. Once, on a subway in New York, a woman hung from a strap and stared at me for a minute, never able to avert her perplexed eyes. When the crowd thinned out, she cocked her head to one side and yelled, "Hey! What's wrong with you, honey?" "Ski jump!" I replied, knowing that she would consider the technical term as a contagious disease. Pleased, she departed with her newly acquired dinner-time anecdote. At another time, while swimming in an Ozark pond, I noticed a farmer standing on the hill with his indifferent mule. He watched, drop-jawed, as I climbed the hill. As I passed him, he blurted, "Ya po' lil' gal! Wot hurt ya?" Considering, I answered, "Kicked by a horse!" I knew that this was a type of tragedy he could understand. And once I got into a taxi with a drunken driver who immediately assumed that I was also inebriated and insisted on driving toward the county taverns. Since my protests did not stop him, I told him that I had epileptic seizures. I was soon dropped at my doorstep like a hot potato.

Sometimes, however, the situation is reversed, and the joke is on me, as the following incident will show. I was walking down the Reforma in Mexico City when I saw an old Indian woman on the corner, staring with frightened eyes at the six-laned traffic. I motioned the traffic to stop with my cane and ushered the old woman across the boulevard. On the opposite side, she firmly refused to let go of me. Having exhausted my Spanish, I explained to a pedestrian who spoke English that I had just helped the woman across the heavy traffic. After a discourse between the two, the old woman howled with laughter. It seems that she hadn't wanted to cross the boulevard but had thought that I did.

I have now grown accustomed to the persistent reminder that I attract the lunatic fringe of society and have accepted this fact. It used to baffle me that so many eccentrics were drawn into the confessional of my studio, but a psychiatrist I know explained it this way: "You may as well get used to it; you are a catalyst. You draw impurities to the surface." People without active interests of their own or without fully developed identities often seek to find, outside themselves, some symbol of the dramatic or tragic or heroic. Perhaps part of the time it is because contact with the weak or injured makes them feel stronger or superior. I have been exploited from time to time as a guilt outlet and at other times as a social foil to dramatize the good deeds of some so-called friends. I was once told by a chronically unhappy friend that she felt jealous of my handicap because I attracted more attention and more unusual people than she could with her uncomplicated situation. I realize now that I have invited some of these situations and that the self in each of us must be dramatized in this era of conformity. The only individualism left is to be handicapped or neurotic. Both conditions together can be discouraging.

Where the causes for certain social attitudes lie so deeply buried and are of so many different kinds, almost all related to the needs of "normal" people rather than to anything that is true and real about ourselves, the handicapped have an unusual social burden to bear. Self-preservation requires learning how to be on guard, how to be as objective as possible in all situations, how to keep a sense of humor if it can, indeed, be kept, how to be gentle in turning away the lunatic fringe—the food faddist, the faith healer, and the others who carry cures about in capsules. With such people who are attracted to my coxcomb of a handicap, I am as gentle as the situation demands, and I try to communicate in the vernacular they can understand. We handicapped also have to learn to protect our rights to our own little greeds and small vices, and especially our right to become exasperated. I have never been able to understand the universality with which the public holds that handicapped people of all kinds should be models of patience and grace. The right to get mad occasionally is something we have to hold out for!

Besides, it is humanly important to experience rejection; some kinds of rejection result, of course, from the show of anger or resentment, but there are other kinds. Every human being, handicapped or not, has to deal with this experience in order to become strong enough to call himself mature. I myself would feel insecure accepting praise and esteem without knowing any honest rejection or candid disapproval.

I am too lazy, too pleasure-loving, too bent on a literary career to fit the image of the crusader. But it is quite true that working for United Cerebral Palsy has added meaning and excitement and satisfaction to my life. Oddly enough, the organization uses my background and training as a writer rather than as a cerebral palsied woman. I work in the public relations division. However, it is a profound desire of mine to use my writing ability directly in a book of my own for those who suffer from cerebral palsy. I am convinced that many withdrawn, embittered, hurt young people (and others who have been spared these severe reactions) can be reached through the written word if it is written directly to them about things they have to deal with. I think the privacy of the reading experience is most valuable in the transmission of hope and courage and knowledge to handicapped people.

Ida B. Levine

Ida B. Levine was born in New York City on July 14, 1906, a victim of athetoid cerebral palsy. She attended Public School 168 in Brooklyn and the Eastern District High School, from which she was graduated in 1925. Knitting and stamp collecting are her major hobbies. Active in a number of charitable organizations, she is on the Advisory Board of the Federation of the Handicapped. At present, Miss Levine is employed as a mail and supply clerk. She is single and lives in Brooklyn.

I live in Brooklyn and work in Manhattan. I drive my own car back and forth, but before I had my car I rode the subways. I didn't start getting about by myself until I was twenty-five years old. It seems to me that everything exciting that has happened to me began when I knew I was able to travel.

In those days we had what we called social clubs. Richman League was one of these clubs to which my friends took me. There I met Dr. Alfred Richman, the club's sponsor, and was very much attracted to him, both personally and because I had a strong feeling he could help me as a doctor. At that time I didn't know I had cerebral palsy.

More than anything, I wanted to talk to Dr. Richman. They were planning a boat ride, and he said he'd give a party for whoever sold the most tickets. I came home very excited. All of my family—my father, mother, brothers, and sisters—bought tickets. I sold more tickets than anyone, well over fifty tickets. Dr. Richman gave the party for me. When I saw him again, I asked him, "Isn't there anything you can do for me?" He told me to come to his office, and I explained to him that I couldn't travel. We talked it over together, and he finally persuaded me that it was possible.

I was to be driven to a subway station and put on a subway. Then I was to be met at the subway station by a taxi, for which Dr. Richman himself paid.

He discovered that one of my knees needed an operation, and the operation was performed. Then the problem of my great wish to travel and my fear of doing it came up in earnest. The desire to get to someone I liked and someone I knew would help me had been the first big step. But Dr. Richman had bigger plans for me. He understood my feelings about wanting to go places. As a girl I used to watch the world go by, and I used to think, "*If I could only, only* go somewhere I want to go *when* I want to go." I don't think anybody could have had a kinder family than mine or more friends who were willing to "take me along." But this is never the same as being able to go where you want to go yourself. Dr. Richman made me realize that this was also important as far as getting a job was concerned. We talked about it a lot, and he made me psychologically ready to try on my own. My mother bought me a cane. Then Dr. Richman said to me, "Well, now travel." He helped me to perform the miracle. After that my mother always said, "First God, then Dr. Richman."

As a child I was never aware of a speech impediment. I didn't know about it until I reached the age of sixteen. At that time I said to my Latin teacher, "I'm going to be operated on; I'm going to a doctor." She said, "Is he going to do anything about your speech?" I didn't know what she meant. I went home and said to my girl friend, "What's wrong with my speech?"

She said, "I dunno. Something wrong with you?"

"I dunno. Imitate me."

She did.

One time I got myself a job canvassing, taking orders for tea and coffee. I traveled to New Jersey and all around by bus and subway. I made a lot of money. I had sympathetic customers. I worked as a canvasser a year and a half. I got very tired. I had taken a civil service exam years before, but of course when I went for an interview, my disability prevented my being appointed. I was always told, "Oh, we'll let you know." Then I thought of politics. I went after the leader of my district, and I pressured him and told him I wanted an interview. Soon the Bureau of Motor Vehicles called me for a job. When I arrived at the office, there were hundreds of people being interviewed. The woman who was interviewing said, "Well, what do *you* want?"

"I've come to work," I answered.

"Well, you can't work," she said.

"But I have this letter saying to come to work."

"But you *can't* work."

"But I have this letter asking me to come to work, and I'm staying right here."

I wouldn't go away. I was very determined. So I stayed all that day and continued with the job. It was only a temporary job, but they were pleased with my work, and I left with good references. And I had learned what it was like to have a real job. In 1932 I was appointed for one month as a clerk with the Temporary Relief Administration. Before the end of the month, my supervisor went to Albany and said he wanted me on his staff. I've been with them twenty-seven years. The Department of Social Welfare took over their functions, and that's where I am now. When I was first hired I made $1800. To me this is the most interesting kind of work possible.

I don't earn much money at my job, but I have another enterprise. I call myself a personal shopper. I sell Christmas cards and greeting cards. I don't canvass and I don't solicit, but some people know about it. During the Women's International Exhibit this year, I took a week of my vacation and sold Christmas cards. I made $100. Anybody who *wants* to do something can—and can earn money.

I had always wanted to drive a car. One day I walked into the Federation for the Handicapped, where New York University had requested space to give a course in driving for handicapped people. I just happened to walk in. I asked an instructor whether or not they could teach me. He inquired of his supervisor and learned that they never taught CP's. I told her that all I wanted was the chance to *see* whether they could teach me to drive. She got one of the instructors to give me a chance. The report came back that they weren't set up for people like me, but that there was a place in Brooklyn. So I went there.

I said, "All I want is a chance to *see* whether or not I can." Then an instructor took me out. He said he couldn't teach me in ten lessons but that if I gave him more time, he thought perhaps I could learn. First I had to have a note from a doctor saying that I would be a safe risk on the highway.

When I spoke to a doctor, I asked him what I could do to better my condition. He said, "Learn to drive a car." And so he sent the note. Then I got my permit and went to school. I said to the instructor, "I give you one year to teach me how to drive a car." It took about four months. The instructor was fine. He used psychology. When he took me out we went a great many places. Once I saw that he was taking me to the bridge. "Oh, I'm not gonna cross the bridge!" "Come on," he said. "You're going to cross the bridge." And so, we crossed the bridge. Anyway, at the end of four or five months he wanted me to take the test. But I waited and took it at the end of nine months. He said, "You're not going to pass, you know, but I want you to know what it's like." He explained that I wouldn't pass because the inspector wouldn't believe I could do it, but he said he thought I was ready for the test. I took it and failed. I took another and failed. I took a third and passed. Then I was a full-fledged driver.

But I took another year of lessons before I drove by myself. I wanted to be sure. I knew now that this was very important to me. I took the lessons instead of going to a doctor. You know, we can't pass anybody when we're walking. We never know the feeling of passing anybody except in a car.

I travel a great deal and I enjoy it. I've been to Canada, Havana, Bermuda, California, Salt Lake City, Los Angeles, Grand Canyon, Pike's Peak, Nova Scotia, Florida. I've visited every part of New York State on weekend bus trips. Next week I'm flying to Miami. I used to make long trips by bus, but now I fly.

I have several hobbies. I collect stamps, and I have some beautiful ones. I do the most gorgeous knitting you ever saw. It's impossible to realize I could turn out such beautiful things. I knitted a sweater with a beautiful design of a man and woman on the front and another with two love birds on it. I used to knit all the time in the subway, but now I can't knit while I'm traveling because, of course, I drive my car. I make all my suits, coats, and heavy dresses.

I love clothes. During the summer I have eighteen or nineteen dresses, and I wear a dress only once every three weeks. Oh, yes, and earrings. I have many pairs of earrings, and never once do my earrings fail to match the dress I'm wearing. I had grey hair, and I loved my grey hair. Then someone dared me to dye it blonde. So I went into a beauty parlor, and now I'm a blonde. The operator said, "But you don't want to do this!" I said I did. She said, "But *why* do you want to?" "Because somebody dared me to." I wash my hair every Saturday morning. I have my own waves—it's naturally curly. I have my nails manicured every week, and I take a shower every night. I think it's important to be well groomed.

I'm a very active person. I drive my sisters wherever they want to go. There's nothing wrong with them, but they just couldn't pass the road test. I'm the chauffeur. I wash and dry dishes, wash and iron my own clothes. People ask me when I find time to do all this, and I say, "Why, at two o'clock in the morning. There's always time then." I read the newspaper every night before I go to bed. And I go out with my friends to movies. I don't drink or smoke, although I don't disapprove of anyone who does. I was given a free rein by my parents, but I simply don't enjoy those things. I have many friends, one who is completely incapacitated. Most people can't understand her at all, but I do pretty well.

I enjoy doing as much as I can for disabled people. I want to do for others. And I don't refuse help myself when I need it. Even able people need help. I would never cross an icy street by myself. I'd say, "Would you mind helping me?" Once not long ago I was carrying a heavy load upstairs, and some young girls came by. I said, "Look, girls, would you like to be my bannister? Just give me your little finger." And they were glad to do so.

So what haven't I got that I need? I don't walk straight, but I get there. The most important things in life are a job, family, and friends. I have them all. The sidewalks are cockeyed—it isn't me. I'm thankful, very thankful.

Joan Hardee

Joan Hardee was born in Denver, Colo., in 1927 but was educated mainly in the East. At the age of twenty-one, she contracted polio. She is now married to a New York lawyer and lives with him and her five children in a five-story Victorian house overlooking the East River. She is active in the March of Dimes, in local politics, and with the school board. For a year, Mrs. Hardee wrote a column on food for a local newspaper.

For twelve years I have lived with polio—more specifically, with paralyzed arms. I have lived with my disability so long, and it is such a part of me, that I forget much of the time that I am crippled. I forget until something or someone reminds me. Recently, a little girl of three, a friend of my three-year-old daughter, asked why I leaned back in such a way (I was reaching for a loaf of bread on a shelf in the market and had to throw my arm up to knock the bread down so that I could pick it up), and why my arms hung down so funny. I answered her that I had been sick a long time ago and that my arms did not work very well any more. My big children usually answer for me, "Oh, that—my mother had polio." This usually ends the conversation.

For my children and for my husband and my close friends, I am what I am not because of polio but in spite of it. Polio did its part in shaping me, just as so many other things in life—the parents who bore me, the events of childhood, genes and chromosomes, protons and atoms, and the soul that was bestowed upon me.

This is not to say that I have not worked hard to get as physically and emotionally well as possible or that having polio does not matter. It matters very much, every day of my life. I only say that

I have come to accept my limitations and they no longer cause me overwhelming grief. The way toward this acceptance of my physical self has not been easy or smooth. I have suffered physical pain and emotional pain and I know I have caused pain in others, but there have been some significant episodes, most of which have put me ahead a few steps at a time.

I became sick with polio when I was twenty-one, an age when I thought the world was turning just for me. I had many petty problems, but I thought they would all be solved just the way I wanted them solved. When I found myself in the hospital desperately ill, all I could think was: "How dare this happen to me?" I had a very strong, conscious wish to die, and I remember begging the doctors (but since I could not move a muscle either to breathe or to speak, it was all in my mind) to leave off the oxygen mask so that I would not have to live. Soon after, when I began to be able to breathe just a bit, I knew that I would not die, and could not, even though I wished it. I slumped into a great depression with no positive wish or will about anything.

I did call upon God to help me, but my conception of God at that time was catch-as-catch-can and tinged with youthful magic. For example, one day I said to myself, "If I hear some particular music (it happened that Beethoven's *Seventh Symphony* was a particular favorite of mine as a child) I shall know that God is somehow going to help me." The next morning, quite early, from down the corridor came the first loud sounds of music. A patient had turned the radio on too loud at first, then more quietly, and there it was—Beethoven's *Seventh Symphony*! I burst into tears and, despite this seeming coincidence, felt, from that moment on, there were perhaps certain things worth living for.

When I got out of the hospital, my arms still hurt a great deal. I had no use of either arm or of my left hand, and very little use of my right hand. I carried both arms in a single sling because it was unbearably painful to let them hang at my sides. After some weeks of pain, I finally went to see a polio specialist to get some pills or treatment to relieve the acute pain. He examined me and did all the muscle tests that had been done so many times before and finally, while I was still sitting on the examining table, he said, "Your right hand will get stronger and you may get a little something back in your right arm, but I doubt it. You will get nothing back in your left arm or your left hand." I felt as though I had been struck a hard physical blow. It took several moments before I was able to think or to speak. "But Doctor," I said at last, "I came to you to get rid of my pain, and anyway no other doctor has told me this."

"You came to me for a diagnosis and for my opinion, and this is my opinion. You must now start living with your disability." After some minutes, when I had recovered from this acute shock, I pointed out to him what I thought were some insurmountable situations. At that time I could not even go to the bathroom by myself. His answer to me was that in order to cope with this problem I would have to do without underpants. I was beside myself with indignation: "Well, I never have and I know I never can!" If I had known then some of the really hard things that I would have to adjust to, I would have realized the triviality of this problem.

I left the office that day a very shaken young woman. I was in a towering rage at this doctor who dared tell me this (he never did give me anything for the pain in my arms), but I was a young woman with a number of new ideas to think about. Even though there were other doctors who later gave me hope of getting somewhat better, I never really believed them. In my heart of hearts I knew this man was right, though I hated him for telling me. Some day I would like to see this doctor and thank him. I have very happily given up several extraneous female garments and am much more comfortable than most conventionally dressed women. We all have so many preconceived ideas of what we must wear, of what we must do and how we must do it. One finds as one goes along that one can do many things in unbelievably different ways. I think, for example, of the morning my three-year-old daughter, copying my method, began making her bed with her feet. One way gets it done about as well as the other.

When I had polio, my oldest daughter (by my former marriage) was two and, at that time, my only child. She was separated from me for three months or more and, when we were reunited, I was not the same Mummy she had known. I could not pick her up or even hold her on my lap. I could not hug her or help her or, in fact, do anything for her. To add to my own grief, my child would not even speak to me. When I called her, she went running from me and screamed for her father. One day she was sitting at the table after having finished her supper and she wanted to get down. She screamed for her Daddy. I said that her Daddy was busy and couldn't come and that I would help her down. I did not know how I was to manage this. She said to me, "You can't, and anyway I want my Daddy." (Luckily for me, her father was taking a shower and could not hear her.) I repeated that her father was busy and that if she wanted to get down, I would help her. I went over to her chair and kicked it away from the table with my foot and then knelt down and told her to put her arms around my neck. With great hesitation and resentment she did this, and I was able to help her slip to the floor. She then wanted her bib off, and again she called for Daddy. I said that I would take her bib off. By this time I was stubbornly determined, although I had very little strength in my right hand. To complicate matters, the bib string was tied in a knot. However, after many minutes of working at the knot (my child stood very still and very patiently, once she was certain that I meant what I said), I finally undid the knot and took the bib from around her neck.

From that moment on, we began to re-establish our proper mother-child relationship. She could again begin to count on me as a functioning and reliable mother, although, in fact, I could not do very much for her physically. It was a long time before I realized that there was much more to being a mother than changing diapers and putting food on the table but, like every other mother with or without a disability, I had to grow up to my womanly tasks in life.

For about a year after polio I was all too busy proving to myself and to the world that I was a pretty courageous person. I was like Roo in *Winnie the Pooh*: Look at me, Roo, look at me doing all these wonderful things. And then, quite without warning, the structure that I had built for myself and the image of myself that I had made broke down. I became overwhelmed by anxiety. I was no longer the courageous me of yesterday. Over a period of several weeks I became increasingly anxious about falling down stairs, about fainting and vomiting, and finally I became too anxious even to leave my own home. I was utterly immobilized by this anxiety. I could not leave my house nor could I remain comfortably inside. I could not go up or down stairs, be with people, or remain entirely alone. At last, with no other place to go and no other help to turn to, I sought out psychiatric help.

Soon after I started psychiatric therapy, the symptoms of my anxiety became much less severe, to a point where I thought that I was cured. It was not so. This was just a temporary surcease, and it was only then that my real work began. I had the work of disentangling all the bits and pieces of my life, polio included, that had led up to this anxiety. I stayed at this work (I say "work" because that is what it was for me—hard, but gratifying, work) for at least four years. There were many moments of the deepest despair and the greatest triumphs. I thought, from time to time, that I would never feel anxious again. But that was not so. I am still anxious at the prospect of the long steel subway stairs—I look down them and wonder whether or not I can make the conscious effort to walk down. Actually, one day I did fall on some steel stairs and gave my chin a hard knock. I had actually fulfilled my anxiety and was alive and not badly hurt.

After that, I was never quite so anxious again. I realized, too, that a little well-placed anxiety was probably a good thing. I am careful, which, when one cannot hold on or brace oneself, is essential. I found, in the process of psychiatric therapy, that polio alone was not the cause of my various anxieties. I found there were many demons of different forms and ferocities, and that polio was one of the triggers that released them. Thinking about this, especially after so many years, I am not sure that psychiatric therapy solved my problems. But it certainly has had its effect in my response to life and has helped me alter some of the paths I had chosen.

Polio has made some profound changes in my life and in the lives of thousands, and no magical thinking is going to alter this fact. Some people still say to me occasionally, "My brother-in-law's cousin had polio and he is just fine." I am glad for the brother-in-law's cousin, but this does not alter one bit my rehabilitation or the conditions of my life. Once upon a time I was a very athletic young woman, rode horseback, played tennis, swam powerfully. I was desperately unhappy right after polio because these joys were to be denied me forever. It took time, but today I am truly happy for those people who can play tennis and I no longer yearn to play myself. I get quite enough exercise chasing after children and I still have the delight of walking and dancing. I have known a few men who were shy about dancing with me because my arms are paralyzed, but my husband contends that I am quite a good dancer (though I suspect him of prejudice in this matter).

As long as I have young children around me (and I suspect I will have grandchildren trailing about before all my children are grown), I will need physical help in the house. It is a serious matter when I do not have help—I cannot change diapers, and I have trouble doing the endless chores and get tired to the point of tears if I have to do all that is demanded without help in the house. In this area, I am dependent, very dependent, and it can be a most frustrating feeling to have to be so, although all people are dependent upon one another in some ways. My children are dependent upon me for their center of gravity. I am dependent upon them and upon my husband and friends for physical and spiritual help as they are dependent upon me for help, friendship, and love.

The machine age has made some great and tangible contributions to my life. I write on an electric typewriter because I haven't the strength to hit the keys of a regular typewriter. There are all sorts of one-handed kitchen devices and, of course, there are always my feet to work with. Recently, I acquired a car with foot steering, and this has given me the greatest freedom and pleasure.

Of all the intangible forces—with such tangible results—in making the human being whole and happy, love is the prime one. There are many kinds of love: love of children, of husband and wife, of close family and friends, and, for many of us, love of God. Soon after we met, my husband said to me, "I think I might not

have fallen in love with you if your arms had not been paralyzed."
Every living person has different needs and desires to be fulfilled
by other people, but that which is common to us all is the need to
be loved. When I first was paralyzed, I thought I was no longer of
any value and therefore not worth loving. How woefully wrong I
was, and selfish, to start from that point of view. I found through
love, and because of love, that one is filled with love not by the
taking but by the giving. One gives and gives of love and eventually
one is filled with it. Love is the most healing force in the world,
and I am certain that discovering how to love deeply was the
most effective way to learn to live with myself and polio.

How dare it happen to me! The world moves in mysterious
ways, and the further and further we probe, the more mysterious
life and the substance of it become. Children think in such simple
terms—things are either fair or unfair—but as we grow up, we must
think along more subtle lines. Many things which happen to us
do not seem justified, but then we do not know the ultimate outcome. At first I thought that it was desperately unjust that I
should have polio; "After all, what did I do to deserve this?" was
my kind of thinking. But it's certain that I never would have
learned any kind of patience without living through polio, never
learned the kind of compassion that comes from suffering, and
probably never known how to love as I hope I know today.

Claire and William Behr

William Behr was born in New York City on August 31, 1911. At the age of five he was stricken with polio. He had no formal rehabilitation until he attended the Institute for the Crippled and Disabled after his graduation from elementary school in 1925. Since 1930 he has worked as a self-employed watchmaker. He married Claire Power in 1940. They now have five children who range in age from three-and-a-half to eighteen. Mr. Behr enjoys fishing and traveling and he is a charter member of the Will and Way Fellowship, an organization designed to help shut-ins. His wife, Claire, was born in New York City on February 19, 1912. Stricken with polio at the age of six, she spent a long time in hospitals. She received office training from the Institute for the Crippled and Disabled in 1932–33. She was employed by the WPA from 1935 to 1940. Married in 1940, she settled down to the life of housewife and mother. She shares her husband's interests and activities.

My husband and I both had polio in the epidemic of 1916, but we didn't meet until the 1930's in New York City. Today we are the proud, happy parents of five healthy children. The years between explain, to my mind, why this story is possible.

We were fortunate to have parents who were courageous and wise enough not to overprotect us. As a mother today, I understand how much courage it takes not to say "Don't" or "You can't." As the oldest of a large family, I was expected to do as much as possible to help. My disability was accepted and never discussed, and, from about the age of twelve, I was permitted to make my own decisions about all my activities because my mother felt that I knew my own limitations. As another example of the value of independence, my husband started to save money for a car when he was fourteen, during a time when ownership of a car was uncommon. When he was nineteen, with the help of his parents, he bought his first car. His mother says today that she never closed her eyes until she heard the car roll into the garage, but she never passed her fears on to her son.

When I first met my husband, he was still filled with the wonder of driving a car, and I knew him for fifteen years before I understood. It took me that long to get up the courage to learn to drive, but once I had my driver's license I regretted the lost years. I discovered that a handicapped person feels the equal of anyone on the road when he is behind the wheel.

I grew up in a small community at a time when there were no educational plans for the handicapped. You got to the neighborhood school somehow or you did without the three R's. To me and my mother, not going to school was unthinkable, and fortunately I was able to walk well enough to get there. Today I know what a tremendous debt I owe to the principal of that school, who advanced me in spite of my losing ground because of accident, illness, or operations, and, believe me, my absentee record was a horror.

I had gone on to another school before I had an inkling of the pressures that the principal had withstood from his superiors, who had opposed his advancement policy. The new principal told me bluntly, "I'm not going out on a limb for you, as he has all these years." Then she promptly "forgot" to inform my teachers that I had been advanced on probation. Later, when I spilled the beans and the teachers protested, her answer was, "I wanted you to give her her chance without prejudice." Without the encouragement these principals gave me during a very important time, I'm sure I would have given up trying, not only to get an education but to make something worth while out of my adult life. My husband lived in New York City, which pioneered in schooling for the handicapped, so his education was better organized.

The Works Progress Administration was a much maligned part of the Depression years, but to many handicapped people it proved to be a godsend. I was employed as a temporary clerical worker during its first days and was assigned to a job that proved more essential than I first thought. It lasted long enough to prove to me that I was as qualified as anyone to handle complicated jobs and to deal with other organizations. This did much to give me the self-confidence I so badly needed, and it made me realize how important a part employment plays in the building up of the morale and self-confidence of handicapped people.

During these Depression days, my husband-to-be was having his troubles getting work as a watchmaker, so he finally opened a small candy store with a watchmaker's bench in one corner. Slowly his trade built up, thanks largely to those people who spread the word of his competence to their friends and fellow-workers. Some men were regular runners, bringing work back and forth from the office or factory, collecting payments, and doing anything they could to help. During World War II, the servicemen, who as tots a few short years before bought penny candy from Bill, remembered him when their watches needed repair, and it wasn't unusual for the postman to bring in small packages from all parts of the world addressed to "Bill's Busy Corner, Whitestone, N.Y." They didn't know his last name or address but they remembered the lettering on his first candy store awning. He was now in a new location a few blocks away, operating a small jewelry store, but the post office never missed. It was always a thrill to get one of those packages.

When we were married, we were determined to live as normally as possible, and that meant children and a home of our own. We first lived in apartments, but near our fifth anniversary we moved into our own home—with two children. With hard work and perseverance my husband makes a comfortable living in a business that he built up with no financial assistance from anyone but with much encouragement and help from family and friends.

Between us, we have ten brothers and sisters. Without exaggeration we can say our lives are the equal of the best of them and better than some. We have much to be grateful for because, as children, neither of us believed happy and normal lives were likely or possible.

Emily Anderson Dodd was born about eighty years ago in Sarnia, a town in Ontario, Canada. As a very young child she began to lose her hearing. After graduating from high school,

Emily Anderson Dodd

she left Canada in order to study nursing in the United States. At the end of her nurse's training, she was married and settled down as the wife of a physician in West Orange, N.J. Dr. Dodd died in 1927, and Mrs. Dodd established a physicians' service and nurses' registry in order to support herself. Although she has decreased the volume of her business, she is still independent and earns her own living.

As I look back over my eight decades, I think now that my hearing was never quite normal. In a big family such as mine, a child is more likely to be thought inattentive or stubborn than deaf. It was an inconvenience to my parents that I did not always listen and obey, and I spent many an hour weeding the kitchen garden because I did not do what I was told to do fast enough. My brothers and sisters more or less took for granted that sometimes I would hear and answer and at other times not join their plots and plans. But no one in my family thought I was stupid, and I could not understand why the teachers sometimes did.

Unspoken accusations began in the first grade. These slights did not happen often, but they hurt my feelings when they did. I could read faster than most of the other children by the time I got through the second grade, and I liked arithmetic and usually had my problems done correctly. When the teacher grew impatient with me, I felt it was unfair. I liked games a lot, but many of the games we played at recess depended on hearing a signal or my name called in the inarticulate excitement of play.

I think I could hear clearly only words which were spoken loudly enough and in a fairly conventional way. Perhaps this means that, without knowing it, I had already begun to lip-read. But, in any case, I was so often confused or blamed in the more active games that I usually stood on the sidelines or played on the swings, which bored me. I was by nature a fairly athletic girl, however, and, as I grew older, tennis became my game. I developed the ability to keep score pretty accurately, but whenever I was wrong I always accepted my opponent's count.

One incident I remember is still a mystery to me. It was almost always a lowered voice that I missed, because I could hear most things when I was a child. But in the third or fourth grade there was a fire drill one day, and I failed to hear the gong. When all the children had filed out of the room, I concluded that the class had been dismissed, and I went home. As far as I know, everyone with any authority over me took some part in the penalties I paid for this. Yet no one, least of all myself, suspected that my hearing was at fault.

I am rather proud of the fact that I never really thought I was stupid. The world was puzzling to me, and the behavior of adults seemed especially unreasonable. But I presumed that the world is puzzling to everybody and I accepted it as I found it from day to day. But after I was grown up, I would never weed a garden.

While my family was making up its mind that I had an unpleasant habit of saying "Huh?" to many things, I myself was coming to some conclusions. I decided that I liked to read and play alone rather than join groups. At least no one could accuse me of trying to get attention when I was sitting on my bed reading Elsie Dinsmore! But as I grew older, this defensive habit made me aware of loneliness, and I tried so hard to make one or two close friends in my teens that I succeeded. Although they are no longer alive, I did have these friends and was grateful to them, and kept in touch with them most of my life.

When I finished high school, the feeling that I wanted to be with people made me decide to go into nursing. Other circumstances also entered into this decision, but one of the main things was that I felt that even a shy and unusually quiet girl could learn to care for the sick and help with the routine work of a hospital.

This was the first of many decisions which have followed the same pattern: I have somehow maneuvered myself into positions where I could be in touch with people without having to take full responsibility for hearing every sound. It was the social situations that grew increasingly difficult, where different people in different positions were saying things in low voices. In training, I knew *where* to listen most of the time—I could watch the doctor's lips, or the supervisor's, or the patient's and not make very many mistakes. At that time I did not consciously know that I had begun to depend on lip reading.

Yet more than once the nurses in charge were impatient with me for not hearing an order, and, of course, in a sick room it is especially likely that words will be spoken in a very low voice. After one such episode, a young intern, Dr. Dodd, discussed the matter with me over coffee the following day and told me, kindly yet positively, that my hearing was quite impaired and that he had been observing for several months the small difficulties I got into from not catching on quickly enough to what was expected of me. I liked him very much, and what he told me led to a crisis of self-knowledge. Suddenly I could see the cause for almost all the sadness and loneliness I had ever known. Or perhaps I should not say "suddenly"; it takes some time to go back over twenty years of misunderstanding.

After I was capped, I was appointed night supervisor for a terminal ward. Although the duty was certainly not a very heartening one, any supervisory position is advantageous to a deaf person who has prepared himself for it. One can more easily learn to arrange things and give orders than one can follow the instructions of others.

Dr. Dodd spent a lot of time beside my desk whenever he was on ward duty at night. He had asked me to marry him, but I had hesitated a long time because, by now, I realized that my deafness was progressive, and it seemed to me this would be a great disadvantage to a doctor's wife. But after a while, I overcame my first doubts and knew that I really wanted to marry him. I kept hoping he would ask me again.

He did, and shortly after we were married we bought a house, had offices and operating rooms attached to the side of it, put up a new shingle, and began to wait for the first patient. My husband was an unusually kind man, and he must have had to reassure me a hundred times during the first year that my deafness did not make me less dear to him.

After the birth of my daughter, my hearing became worse, and when my son was born, the loss was still greater. My husband was concerned about it, but neither his own knowledge nor that of specialists to whom I went was sufficient to account for the cause or to suggest any treatment for a condition which was worsening rapidly. My family adjusted to my deafness quite casually, as children are likely to adjust to whatever happens to a parent.

When my husband died in 1927, my children were grown up, and I had also lost my best friend. I felt pretty intensely the extreme loneliness of the handicapped person for whom doctors can do nothing and for whom, so often, the world makes no place, not even a small one. It took me two or three years to think things out.

I believe that a person's knowledge of what he can and cannot do is vital to his happiness and welfare. He should *think* about this before following the suggestions of other people. My own decision about what to do was based on what I had known all along: I could be most useful in a supervisory capacity and I could deal with my almost total deafness only when talking to one person at a time. It is a strange, unnatural feeling to listen as hard as you can and to be able only to guess at what is going on.

My granddaughter had a psychology text in college which stated that deaf people are likely to be suspicious. I believe that this is a kind of error in understanding. One has to do a good deal of guessing at times in order to account for what has not been explained. Some of this guessing is done to account for disappearances or absences or losses—guessing that can easily be mistaken for suspicion.

Actually, I think it could be affirmed that deaf people learn to *trust* more than others have to. When I take off my hearing aid at night, all the fire alarms in the city could not wake me, and my home could be burglarized at leisure without my knowledge. I have to spend more than half my time quite without the protection that hearing provides. To a greater or less extent this is true of all deaf or partially deaf people—more than others, they have to trust and rely upon their own abilities to work out a good life.

In 1907, while still an infant, Edward Kafka contracted polio, which left him with total paralysis of both legs, a weakness in his left arm, and curvature of the spine. Since his graduation from high

Rose and Edward Kafka

school, Mr. Kafka has operated his own stationery store and worked for an interior decorator and as a technician in the manufacture of lenses and other optical instruments. He is currently employed as a color photo technician. Among his numerous hobbies are traveling, fishing, gardening, bird-watching, and listening to music. He helped organize and is still very active in the Will and Way Fellowship, an organization of disabled men and women devoted to helping shut-ins. His wife, Rose, also contracted polio as an infant. The disease produced paralysis in both legs, curvature of the spine, and a weakness in her right arm. She now walks on braces and crutches, and, besides driving a car, uses all regular modes of transportation. For the past twenty-five years, she has been employed at the Institute for the Crippled and Disabled in New York City, first as a secretary and later as a registrar. She shares most of her husband's interests and also enjoys cooking and baking. In addition to her work in the Will and Way Fellowship, she does volunteer work for the Red Cross.

My husband and I have been disabled since early childhood as a result of polio. Our combined disabilities result in residuals in both legs and a weakness in my husband's left arm and a weakness in my right arm. As an outcome of this, we have found from our experience that, between us, we have one good pair of hands and are able to accomplish almost as much as a nonhandicapped person simply by pooling our resources.

We have thus been able to overcome many of the purely mechanical difficulties that confront handicapped people. Perhaps some of the emotional adjustments have been harder to make. It took a long time for me to be able to face the stares and comments of little children. Generally they point a finger, calling the attention of their playmates to what they see, or ask their mothers all sorts of questions. Mothers will often become embarrassed and pull their child away, adding insult to injury. There have been times, I must admit, when this kind of situation has angered me to the point of vindictiveness.

We can't help noticing the "sympathetic pity" of adults, too. A perfect stranger sometimes approaches and admires you for whatever you may be doing—sometimes simply window shopping, going to a theater, even basking in the sunshine. It has taken time to learn that people really mean to be kind and deserve a friendly response. My husband and I share many interests and hobbies which remove us from some of the tension-creating conflicts. At our small cottage on Long Island, where we spend weekends about six months of the year, we are able to indulge in a variety of interests and accomplish what almost seem like insurmountable tasks simply by working them out to fit our particular needs.

We are especially interested in gardening and canning. We grow sufficient quantities of vegetables to supply our needs for the winter. In view of the necessity of using braces and crutches, bending over to weed, cultivate, and so forth could be almost an impossible task. However, my husband fortunately is mechanically minded and ingenious. He planned and built an electric tractor to fit our needs. It is equipped with a three-quarter horsepower electric motor and a hundred-foot wire cable. The reasons we use electricity rather than gasoline are that there is no problem in starting the tractor and that it is economical, runs constantly, and is instantly reversible. We plotted out our garden patch so that the rows were wide enough to run the tractor through. We can sit on the tractor, which is rather low to the ground, can tend the vegetables, pick them, and carry our produce on it as well.

The tractor is used in dozens of other ways. It carries articles from place to place on our property and is even used as a bulldozer in knocking over small bushes and stumps. We even have an outlet on it, so we can use electric appliances for outdoor cooking.

We do our own painting, decorating, and repairing in our cottage. We have worked out a method of painting ceilings and walls simply by placing a large sturdy platform on wooden horses, putting a chair on the platform, and sitting on it to paint. Where we have closets above reaching height, we have placed handles in the walls so that we can grab them to climb on a chair to reach above. At one time we built a storehouse. Realizing that using a ladder was a physical impossibility for us, we simply built each side of the building by sitting on the ground, and then we had someone put the framework up on the foundation.

We have a car equipped with hand controls and have traveled many thousands of miles over the country. We have found that staying at motels is ideal for the disabled because they are generally level to the ground. The slippery, icy streets in midwinter are a bugaboo for a person on crutches, but we have worked out this problem by keeping a pail of sand in the car, and when we get to our destination we take a bagful of sand and throw it ahead so that we can manage on ice with less hazard.

As I look back over the many years of growing up and learning how to cope with my handicaps, I realize how hard I fought against accepting my limitations, pushing myself to go out in all kinds of weather, perhaps feeling ill enough to stay home but thinking that if I gave in, people would mark me an invalid. Now that I am a little older, I feel less compelled to prove my capabilities. It is a relief to recognize and admit to physical limitations. I think we have learned how to accept help graciously. When my neighbors ring my bell on a snowy day to inquire if I need something from the store, even though I am prepared for bad weather I try to think up some item rather than reject a generous offer. It is kinder to accept help than refuse it in an effort to prove independence.

My husband and I have our particular problems with our handicaps, but there is usually a way of solving them. By depending on each other, we find we need not be deprived of many pleasures. Sometimes it takes a great deal more effort and time than the average person spends, but it is satisfying when we have achieved something by our own efforts.

Domenica Diodati

Domenica Diodati was born in Italy and came to this country at the age of five. Her family settled in Far Rockaway, N.Y., where they still live. Miss Diodati received her high school diploma from the New York Institute for the Blind. She is, at present, a member of the Dramatic Group at the Lighthouse and lives in New York at the Catholic Center for Women. She is employed as a typist.

The deterioration of my retinas was gradual but steady throughout my childhood, and when the process had taken its course I had no vision. This was hard on me and everyone who cared about me because it seemed that every effort to do anything about it failed and discouraged us more each time. It was hard for me in school, trying to keep up with sighted children, often making embarrassing mistakes, and my father lost many days of work taking me from clinic to clinic in his effort to find out if anything could be done to cure or halt the trouble.

I think the first realization of my situation, and the first intense grief resulting from this realization, came one day, very casually, when a group of us in our early teens had gone to the beach for the day. I was lying on the sand, and I guess the fellows and girls thought I was asleep. One of the fellows said, "I like Domenica very much, but I would never go out with a blind girl." I cannot think of any prejudice which so completely rejects you. I felt badly hurt by this, but I have grown accustomed to it as it has kept hurting during the years since then.

It is not unusual for me to have to stand on a bus while people around me discuss my blindness. People quite often assume that if a person is blind he is also deaf. And many times we are treated as

186

though we can't think clearly. When a person finds out that I cannot see the number on a bus, he will often ask me where I want to go. What this chiefly affects is just plain everyday happiness. Most blind people are especially glad to be able to hear and feel and think, and when people deny you these human faculties, you feel awfully discouraged. Even people who try to be nice to you often make it plain how different they think you are. I know that blindness *is* different from vision, but there is a whole lot of a human being that stays the same when one sense fails.

There are very few people who can accept blindness naturally, just for what it is: not being able to see. It is so important to us to be allowed to do what we know we can do independently, not to be questioned as though we were children every time we do something that a sighted person cannot understand our capacity to do. If people would let me do everything I know I *can* do, I would feel more free to ask for help when I really need it. Some people are frightened by blindness; some are morbidly fascinated; some simply forget. People who know blind people are most likely to be understanding. Many people think that blindness is the worst handicap, but I am not so sure. Many handicapped people, including the blind, feel that this is not true.

Once—a few years ago—I thought that I would much rather go out with a sighted man than with a blind man. But I have dates off and on, and slowly my feelings about this have changed. I value the understanding of the blind for the blind, and now I could respect a blind man for his own qualities and be glad for the understanding he could give to me.

Blindness has not changed my social life much. At the Catholic Center, many of the women are blind. I feel at home among the ones my own age, and many of the older ones are kind. I go home about once a month and enjoy seeing my family.

My first jobs were in film companies—doing practically everything to films that can be done. I worked in the darkroom for a while. I was pretty proud of myself when I got my first few pay checks, but the charm wore off. I know I am lucky to have the good job I have now, but even so I wish for a fuller life than the one I lead. From the work point of view, I know I could take more responsibility. From the personal point of view, I suppose I feel that a woman is happiest in a home with husband and children.

Some of my friends are sighted and some are blind. This, somehow, seems to me the way it ought to be—I cannot understand regulating human relations one way or another. No one person stands out in my life as a helper. I suppose the Catholic Church has this place, although my entire family are devout Catholics and I do not think that I am more devout because of my blindness. My parents permitted me to live at the Catholic Center for Women because it is run by nuns. And the sisters are wonderful. They help us all in many ways.

At first I hated to ask for help at any time. It really gets pretty clear that some people just don't want to be bothered, and it isn't always easy to know which ones these are. And some people are just plain embarrassed by being with a blind person. But most people are nice to me; as soon as they find out that I can't see, they become a big help in practical and sensible ways. This is much better than being oversympathetic. Children are usually kind, and I never mind the sort of curiosity they have.

The thing that gives me most confidence—and most willingness to accept help—is the feeling that someone is really trying to understand what I need. When I feel a person is really trying to know something about me, I feel glad to accept his help.

Postscript

As we pointed out in the Introduction, it was our hope that the narratives making up this book would offer the reader a realistic perspective on the problems of the physically handicapped. To that end, we presented the stories of thirty-three handicapped people, none of whom is outstanding or famous, none of whom has acquired great social prominence or unusual material success. Although several of our contributors are above average in both insight and articulateness, they, too, can be considered average in status.

On the whole, then, our contributors lead what must, for want of a better term, be called "ordinary" lives. Most of them speak of their desire for more adequate schooling, their dissatisfaction with their jobs, their loneliness; all of these are "normal" problems, but our contributors have been forced to meet them with the additional obstacles of being without sight, without mobility, without the use of their arms.

Maintaining a stable family life, to take an obvious example, is a most important problem to any married woman, but a woman like Joan Hardee must meet that problem with certain difficulties that the nonhandicapped woman simply does not have to think of. This is offered as a simple fact, not to create out of Joan Hardee (or any of the other contributors) a stereotype combining the selfless devotion of Florence Nightingale with the passion of Albert Schweitzer; such an attitude is actually belittling, for it demands that Joan Hardee become part of that very artificiality she spends her time fighting; it destroys her equality as a human being by insisting that she be interested, body and soul, in truth, justice, selfsacrifice, and virtue. Above all, it imposes upon her a responsibility to the world at large.

189

The idea that handicapped persons are somehow inherently more generous than nonhandicapped persons must be dismissed as the kind of sentimentalized, almost mystical, cliché that is so frequently substituted for intensive analysis and thought. Nevertheless, the simple fact that most of our contributors have been so dependent upon others offers a logical basis for the fact that many of them regard the opportunity to help others as among their deepest satisfactions. Let us, however, accept this satisfaction for what it is—an opportunity for the man who has been served to serve. To point this out does not in any way belittle either the generosity or the motivation of our contributors. One could analyze why individuals take up medicine, law, teaching, or plumbing in much the same manner.

Some of our contributors quite obviously were unable to break away from certain public conceptions of what the handicapped individual is. Some were enervated by a creed which confuses the admission of pain with the "sin" of self-pity. Many of their manuscripts, including almost all that were rejected, dealt with a handicap in the most blandly optimistic, honeyed tones and treated total blindness, for example, with the same "grin and bear it" fortitude with which most people speak about a toothache. Although the original purpose of this book was conceived in reaction against just such an attitude, a few such manuscripts have been included simply because they do represent an attitude toward a handicap which may be more widespread than any other.

Many handicapped persons seem to believe that self-pity is akin to moral cowardice. But some point to it as a potential contributing factor toward a successful rehabilitation. One can recognize this in Leonard Kriegel's account of the personal crisis through which he passed when he realized that he was to be permanently crippled; one can see it in Sandra Noddin's account of her desire to break out of the tight little world of the blind; and one can feel it beneath the hard dignity of Moses Singleton's story. This is not to imply, of course, that self-pity is necessarily desirable. It does, however, suggest that, consciously or unconsciously, self-pity can be turned to advantage.

The handicapped person has also to contend with loneliness—perhaps the greatest of all social and psychological threats in the United States today. Even when loneliness is obvious, many people have difficulty admitting it to themselves, much less to others. And many handicapped people, faced with the prospect of making so basic an admission, choose rather to deny their loneliness. The handicapped person, after all, is a member of his society, and he derives his values, goals, and satisfactions from the same cultural milieu as the nonhandicapped. Some of the contributors—along with a great many others whose manuscripts had to be marked "omit"—refuse to admit that the possession of a severe physical handicap is any reason whatsoever for a person to be lonely. But others speak quite candidly about their isolation. Doris Lorenzen, for instance, does not mention much of the physical pain or loneliness which she has been forced to endure, but she neither avoids nor denies them. Loneliness is there, stamped on every page of her story, but rather than tell us about it, rather than label it, she permits us to see the long months in a hospital, the long ensuing months in a bed at home. And she permits us to see this truthfully, tracing her experiences with both restraint and incisiveness, conveying both the pain and loneliness through which she passed.

Some of our contributors are obviously bitter about what they have experienced. It is not, after all, easy for a person with a physical handicap to avoid bitterness. When a professional musician loses his sight, when a high school athlete finds himself permanently confined to a wheelchair, when an adolescent girl is unable to apply make-up to her face because she cannot control the spasms in her arms, there is a more than sufficient basis for personal bitterness. And yet the very admission of such bitterness, whether it is based in reality or is used by the handicapped person as a psychological weapon to deny his own personal failure, poses still another problem. Bitterness, like loneliness, is no longer part of the acceptable canon of personal feelings in the United States. Thus, the handicapped person finds himself presented with another social taboo—one that insists that he express his pain, his desires, his hopes, and his anguish only in the most superficial manner; if he expresses his bitterness deeply or with any sense of personal tragedy, he risks alienating the nonhandicapped.

The handicapped person who alienates the nonhandicapped may find himself socially isolated. For, although there are many exceptions, most nonhandicapped persons find themselves confused and embarrassed in a social situation with, for example, a victim of cerebral palsy. The easiest way for them to deal with their own reactions is to drop some ostensibly light-hearted remark about handicaps in general. Thus, the nonhandicapped person, seeking to protect himself, insists on keeping the relationship as superficial as possible. The handicapped person, on the other hand, enters into the relationship with great anxiety, wondering how much of a barrier to any real social intercourse his handicap will be. When he finds that the relationship is expected to be superficial, his anxiety increases. A number of such superficial relationships may even induce him to withdraw as much as possible from the society of nonhandicapped individuals.

Harold Yuker, in speaking about how he views his own handicaps, writes:

> In my opinion, people are people, and whether they are
> black or white; Catholic, Jewish, Mohammedan, or
> Protestant; disabled or nondisabled, is immaterial.

This statement provides an excellent example of the attitude that nonhandicapped people believe they should maintain in their relationships with handicapped people. It is, for one thing, highly democratic, for it implies a basic equality between all men in social relationships. But it also denies, by implication, that the handicapped individual is handicapped.

As long as the handicapped individual is cheerful and light-hearted, he is, like the "jolly fat boy," usually accepted by his peers. But let him hint that it is difficult to live without sight, that it is infuriating to want to eat a meal quickly and find that he is physically unable to do so, that it is impossible to conceal sexual desire simply because his legs will not respond to his will, and he is likely to find that his audience is nervously avoiding his eyes, that a few embarrassed coughs have now taken the place of laughter, and that what is flashing across the television screen has suddenly become a focal point of interest.

The truth is that, in most cases, whether one is "disabled" or "nondisabled" is not only material but is frequently *the* decisive factor in social relationships between handicapped and nonhandicapped individuals. Many handicapped individuals have been rejected by their peers simply because their handicaps caused these peers extreme discomfort. On the other hand, some handicapped people have found themselves the object of attention because of their handicap and have succeeded in exploiting this in social situations. Bonnie Jane Garrett tells us of her friend who "felt jealous of my handicap because I attracted more attention and more unusual people than she could with her uncomplicated situation." She then goes on to admit that she "dramatized" her condition as a cerebral palsy victim. Few handicapped people are themselves capable of seeing this, much less admitting it. But the fact remains that many of them actively *exploit* their disabilities, although, since the process is usually unconscious, most of them would probably indignantly deny it.

This kind of social exploitation of a handicap is integrally related to the cultural stereotype of pity for the underdog that has become prevalent in the United States. It can often be a useful stereotype in that it underlies many of our efforts to improve the conditions of the poor, the sick, and the socially rejected. But what such a stereotype does to the individual battling the effects of a physical handicap is another matter. The polio patient, the man with arthritis, the woman with cerebral palsy, the child who loses his sight—all are victims of public relations techniques which stimulate in the public that cloying sentimentality so well represented in mammoth telethons. One wonders whether any of the people responsible for fund-raising in this country have ever imagined themselves in the place of, say, an adult man with cerebral palsy watching a telethon designed to raise funds for the prevention and cure of cerebral palsy. If he has any sensitivity whatsoever, such a "show" forces him to retreat yet further into himself; it adds to his fund of pain and increases his reservations about coming into contact with nonhandicapped people. It informs him that acceptance in the outside world depends upon his willingness to make of himself a pathetic creature—and to remain one so as to serve as the underdog that so many people find necessary. Such programs are ostensibly designed to help him, but the alleviation of human suffering seems to have been lost in the rather revolting antics of such Hollywood "personalities" as Jerry Lewis.

And so, if the handicapped individual does attempt to take advantage of his handicap, is he to be blamed? Our newspapers, magazines, books, motion pictures, and television dramas all beat a constant tattoo of how some individual exploited his "personality" in order to achieve success. If he is able to exploit the fact that he walks on braces and crutches, is not the polio victim acting in accordance with the "image" of him that has been projected by the campaigns of the March of Dimes? His braces and crutches may be considered a part of, or at least an expression of, his "personality," just as the gray flannel suit expressed Madison Avenue's "image" of its own success. We have come so far in projecting images of human beings that it may even be that the victim of a physical handicap should be actively encouraged by occupational therapists to take advantage of his handicap, just as he is taught to compensate for weakness in one part of the body with strength in the other.

The handicapped person is frequently asked to take comfort in such rehabilitation clichés as: "All people are handicapped." Like most clichés, this one has a certain undeniable validity. But is the fact that some people have crooked teeth or childhood scars of any real comfort to, for example, a man whose total blindness has chained him to a transcribing machine? Again, what we are confronting is an attempt to minimize a handicap, an attempt made more in the interest of the nonhandicapped individual than of the handicapped. To assert that handicapped and nonhandicapped face similar psychological problems is to substiute a wasteful kind of sentimentality for constructive thought. Braces on one's teeth simply are not the same as braces on one's legs, and no amount of rationalization will change that fact.

Frequently the handicapped person is forced to pretend that he is not aware of his handicap. A number of the narratives in this book either state this attitude explicitly or imply it. The denial of a handicap as a handicap was even more prevalent in the large number of rejected manuscripts. One potential contributor wrote, "Being blind is not a handicap. My life is exactly like that of other people." This statement stands not, obviously, as truth but as an excellent example of what a culture responsive to Hollywood confuses with courage. Unfortunately, such an attitude is frequently encouraged by the rehabilitation practitioner who, in his desire to help the patient with his physical needs, may overzealously subscribe to this kind of "courage" and use it as an example of what is desirable. But most handicapped people, when learning to combat their handicaps, must face such an attitude with awe and bewilderment; it is a denial of their own suffering and pain, an implication of some sort of moral cowardice on their part.

The patient's lack of awareness of the permanence of his handicap is among the most important problems facing the rehabilitation practitioner. He must attempt to help his patient *adjust to* a physical condition that is usually permanent, but he finds that his patient is not aware of its permanence. Thus, he may be put in the difficult position of first discouraging his patient in order eventually to encourage him. Such an approach may easily lead both to confusion and to psychological tension on the part of the patient, for he is never quite sure of where he stands.

And yet, the lack of awareness of a handicap is often surreptitiously encouraged even by those who are professionally responsible to the handicapped: doctors, therapists, rehabilitation practitioners, social workers, all are sometimes guilty of taking the easy way out, of placating a patient's anxieties rather than attempting to guide him to take a realistic view of himself and his situation. Much of this is undoubtedly done with the patient's welfare in mind; but much of it is nonetheless destructive. The situation in which the doctor finds himself is especially difficult. It is his job to be the first to alert the patient to the possibility of permanent handicap; and one runs across numerous handicapped people who are especially embittered toward members of the medical profession for what they consider to be negligence. "It was a *whole year*," said a young accountant who had been seriously crippled in an accident, "*a whole year* before I could find out that I was paralyzed for good. During those damned long months in bed, I could have been thinking out a lot of things, thinking them out and then thinking them out better. As it was, I had to make new decisions on a new basis all at once, and at the same time that I had to begin work and a new way of living."

The physician, however, is in a quandary of his own, one that the patient does not usually consider. For one thing, it is not always possible to render a long-term prognosis until a considerable amount of time after the initial injury has elapsed; for another, the physician must choose what he feels is the correct moment to inform a patient that the injury is permanent. What the patient may see as an arbitrary and unfair decision may actually be the result of a great deal of contemplation. Perhaps the young accountant's bitterness was justified, but it is also possible that, had the physician informed him of his condition immediately, he would have fallen victim to something far more intense than bitterness—despair.

Overprotective parents, friends, relatives, and acquaintances, usually acting with the best of intentions, can make the road to adjustment even more difficult to travel than it ordinarily is. They stress the concept of "normalcy"; they insist that the cerebral-palsied child demonstrate that he is "as good as anybody else"; they encourage the polio victim to participate in activities in which he can function only as an embarrassment to his friends and to himself; and they do all of this in the belief that they are helping that individual to "adjust to reality."

What this approach fails to take into account is the culture within which the handicapped person functions. It is one thing, for example, for a young boy in an orthopedic hospital to play wheelchair basketball—it is quite another thing for that boy's mother or father to insist that he play basketball in a wheelchair with a group of physically sound friends. In the first case, he is participating in an athletic function that is part of an established norm. In the second he can function only as an object of pity or embarrassment or even secret ridicule; rules must be changed for his benefit, and his presence imposes a strain upon his friends; he becomes a "grotesque," valued by his peers not for his own talents as an individual but for a certain psychic gratification he gives them—the feeling of having done something "good" in permitting him to play. And this attitude is unconsciously encouraged by a public brought up to savor the vicarious thrills of cheap melodrama. In our tabloids, we are confronted by pictures of a post-polio *sitting* on a pitcher's mound to participate in a baseball game; on television, we are greeted by "This Is Your Life" triumphs of saccharine sentimentality; on radio, disk jockeys speak, in tones properly reverent and somber, of how they learned the "true meaning of courage" from listening to a seven-year-old blind girl.

All of this leads one to wonder what it is that the physically handicapped individual should adjust to. Is he, in his search for a life of his own, to latch onto the hole offered him by society, to make his bed in a flotsam of sensationalism, to play the clown to his own pathos? Or is he, rather, to try to equip himself with certain basic substitutes for what he has lost physically, to be his own man, who demands no other excuse for his existence? It is easy enough to nod one's affirmation to the latter, but the choice itself is not that easy. The former role, although it robs the handicapped individual of dignity, does guarantee him a modicum of satisfaction; he is accepted by others, is part of a group, is granted if not self-respect at least the right to exist. He is not, in short, overly embarrassing to others. This may not be a role to be envied, but *it is* a role. But if he demands the right to be his own man, if he insists on living according to his own definition of what is right or wrong for him, then he must run the risk of alienation. He must face the prospect of going it alone, and he must do so in a country that is not, despite what our magazines tell us, filled with admiration for the independent man.

The belief that many handicapped people have of being employed at less than capacity is, as we have pointed out earlier in the book, another two-pronged problem. On the one hand, the belief is frequently justified; handicapped people, like Negroes and other minorities, are often the victims of a none-too-subtle prejudice. On the other hand, the very existence of such a prejudice enables the handicapped individual, again like the Negro or the member of another minority group, to rationalize personal failure by blaming it upon an outside source. But this rationalization, too, seems to be part of our cultural ethos: many nonhandicapped people, if not most, when questioned, would probably claim—and not always with justification—that they, too, are not employed at capacity, that their work is undervalued.

What we have said about employment is equally true of education. Again, the handicapped person, when he verbalizes his desire for an education, is operating in terms of the general cultural ethos. This desire goes hand in hand with the desire to better oneself, and both are indigenous to handicapped and nonhandicapped alike. But the handicapped person does have to face, as we have already shown, a number of difficult and special problems in order to acquire an education, especially a college education. Because colleges and universities are generally conservative, many of them resist the admittance of handicapped persons. This fact may account, at least in part, for the disproportionate academic success of those handicapped students who do manage to go to college.

The decision to compete in school with nonhandicapped students requires unusual personal deliberation and perhaps even professional advice. The handicapped student must recognize that many achievements will take him much longer than the nonhandicapped student; frequently he comes to college with inadequate secondary school preparation; many of the usual areas of college activity are barred to him; he may find that certain courses, such as laboratory sciences, offer insurmountable physical obstacles. But with all this, he usually has a great impetus to succeed in his academic work. For a college education is, at its best, a question of intelligence and sensitivity rather than one of physical prowess. And despite the numerous physical obstacles that it poses for a handicapped individual, the fact is that long-distance runners are not better equipped to solve problems in calculus than are amputees, that Shakespeare can be just as appealing to a victim of cerebral palsy as to a gymnast, and that an individual in a wheelchair can derive as much intellectual satisfaction from reading Spinoza as one who can walk. Most of our contributors who did manage to go to college found the process of learning enjoyable and stimulating, for it granted them greater equality than did most of their nonacademic activities.

As we stated in the Introduction, it was not our intention to offer a "definitive" approach to the problems involved in rehabilitation. But it would be foolish to deny that, as a result of the material collected in this book, we have been led to question a number of current rehabilitory practices and beliefs. There appears, just to cite the most obvious example, to be a lack of integration among different aspects of rehabilitation; and it would seem that a strenuous effort to relate physical, psychological, and vocational rehabilitation needs to be made. In many of the cases included here, no such effort was made; in others, any mode of rehabilitation was haphazard and hit-or-miss.

So many other problems have been raised that it would be impossible to go into them here. But the basic and most difficult problem deserves mention. The split between what the handicapped person wants for himself—a life in which he functions as a responsible and equal member of society—and what our national culture is prepared to give him—a charitable but decidedly second-class right to exist—appears to be growing. Exactly what the solution to this problem is, we do not pretend to know, but it is time that more thought was given to it. And it is not only the handicapped person who must think about it, but rehabilitation practitioners, educators, physicians, psychologists, employers, fund-raisers, and, above all, the much-heralded man in the street. The good society, after all, is that society which can afford to grant all its members the right to be human with dignity.